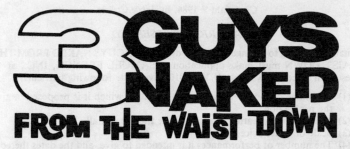

A New Musical

Book and Lyrics by
Jerry Colker

Music by
Michael Rupert

Orchestrations by
Michael Starobin

Originally Directed by
Andrew Cadiff

Winner of Drama Desk Award
Best Book of a Musical 1984–1985

SAMUEL FRENCH, INC.
45 WEST 25TH STREET   NEW YORK 10010
7623 SUNSET BOULEVARD   HOLLYWOOD 90046
LONDON   *TORONTO*

MINETTA LANE THEATRE

James B. Freydberg, Stephen Wells, Max Weitzenhoffer
in association with Richard Maltby, Jr.
present

3 Guys Naked From The Waist Down

A New Musical

Book and Lyrics by
Jerry Colker

Music by
Michael Rupert

with

Scott Bakula   Jerry Colker   John Kassir

Scenery and Projections by	Costumes by	Lighting by	Sound by
Clarke Dunham	Tom McKinley	Ken Billington	Tony Meola

Orchestrations by
Michael Starobin

Musical Director/Conductor
Henry Aronson

Production Stage Manager
Brian Kaufman

Associate Producers
Ray Larsen
Karen Howard

Choreography by
Don Bondi

Directed by

Andrew Cadiff

Originally Presented at PlayMakers Repertory Company, Chapel Hill N.C.

ORIGINAL CAST RECORDING ON POLYDOR RECORDS, CASSETTES AND COMPACT DISCS
Manufactured and Marketed by PolyGram Records

CAST
(in order of appearance)

Ted Klausterman .... SCOTT BAKULA
Kenny Brewster .... JOHN KASSIR
Phil Kunin .... JERRY COLKER

Place: New York City and Southern California

UNDERSTUDIES
Understudies never substitute for listed players unless a specific announcement for the appearance is made at the time of the performance.

For Ted Klausterman and Phil Kunin—Peter Samuel; for Kenny Brewster—Marcus Olson.

MUSICAL NUMBERS
ACT ONE
KOMEDY KLUB EAST
Promise of Greatness .... Ted
Angry Guy/Lovely Day .... Phil
Promise of Greatness (Reprise) .... Ted
THE LAST STAND-UP
Don't Wanna Be No Superstar I .... Ted, Phil
Operator .... Kenny
Screaming Clocks (The Dummies Song) .... Ted, Phil, Kenny,
Mr. Dirtball, Spike, Steve
THE FUNNY FARM
Don't Wanna Be No Superstar II .... Ted, Phil, Kenny
The History of Stand-Up Comedy .... Ted, Phil, Kenny
Dreams of Heaven .... Kenny
FLIGHT 737
Don't Wanna Be No Superstar III .... Ted, Phil, Kenny
Kamikaze Kabaret .... Ted, Phil, Kenny

ACT TWO
The American Dream .... Ted, Phil, Kenny
What a Ride I .... Ted, Phil, Kenny
"Hello, Fellas" Theme .... Ted, Phil, Kenny
"Hello Fellas" TV Special World Tour .... Ted, Phil, Kenny
What a Ride II .... Ted, Phil, Kenny
What a Ride III .... Ted, Phil, Kenny
"Three Guys Naked From the Waist Down" Theme .... Ted, Phil, Kenny
Screaming Clocks (Reprise) .... Ted, Phil, Kenny
Don't Wanna Be No Superstar (Reprise) .... Ted, Phil, Kenny
Dreams of Heaven (Reprise) .... Kenny
I Don't Believe in Heroes Anymore .... Ted
Promise of Greatness (Final Reprise) .... Ted

MUSICIANS
Musical Director/Conductor — **Henry Aronson;** Keyboards — **Paul Sullivan;** Electric Bass — **Seth Glassman;** Drums & Percussion — **Glenn Rhian;** Trumpet—**Phil Granger;** Woodwinds I—**Rick Heckman;** Woodwinds II—**Bob Keller;** Guitar (Electric & Acoustic)—**Brian Koonin.**

Orchestra Contractor—Seymour Red Press

5

DIRECTOR'S NOTES

The heart and soul of *3 GUYS NAKED FROM THE WAIST DOWN* takes place in the comedy clubs. That is where the three guys feel the most comfortable, are able to fully express themselves, and where they establish and ultimately reaffirm their identities. In these club scenes, the show should have an almost improvisational feel. Though the show must be staged and executed like a fine tuned machine, the end result must be a theatricality that is spontaneous, unexpected, and consistently on the edge.

The actors must make the comedy their own, particularly in their opening monologues. Ted must always exercise the freedom to ad lib and improvise. Audiences will vary widely from night to night, and Ted must be ready for anything. He must never shy away from including the audience. They are a crucial part of the evening. It is Ted's responsibility to invite them in. Phil's monologue, because it is set to music, is more precise; but Phil's outbursts — to Kenny, to Ted, to the audience — must be real and make the audience temporarily ill at ease. "Is something wrong on stage?" If the audience asks this question, Phil has succeeded. Kenny's monologue is the most flexible of the three. Certain sound effects and impersonations indicated in the script might be out of the actor's repertoire. Kenny's monologue, as written, is several minutes too long. The actor should be selective, and embellish based on his own specific talents and abilities. The tragic and childlike throughline is essential, however. Note the obsession with images of death and destruction — the grotesque juxtaposition of the gruesome and childish. In general, throughout the show, if the comedy or the choreography are rigid or mechanical, the guys lose their credibility as the total creators of the evening being presented — which is the ultimate effect to strive for.

Scenically, fluidity is the key. The show can never stop moving. A basic club unit, with different backings that change from scene to scene, is essentially all that is required. The scenery, except for the clubs, should be suggestive, not realistic. There should be, however, a strong effect to recreate a club atmosphere as accurately as possible. Bring the show as close to the audience as the theatre will allow, even if it means construct-

6

ing bleachers or extra seating that breaks up a conventional theatrical setting. Though projections were employed extensively in the original New York production (three large screens were used), the show can work without them, or with modified usage. (Subsequent international and national productions used one screen). With the exception of the World Tour and the "Hello Fellas" sequences, projections were used merely as background or embellishment. With clever and resourceful stage management or additional scenic concepts, projections could be eliminated altogether. An added dimension to the scenic design is having the band visible and on stage, preferably set above the main playing area or off to the side.

A successful production finally rests with the three guys and their performances, and thus, the show should work in a cabaret as well as a one thousand seat theatre. The show is about their talent, their dreams, and their friendship. The physical production can be as bare as the guy's souls or as elaborate as their whirlwind journey of success, disillusionment, and finally, self-discovery.

Andrew Cadiff

CAST

(In order of appearance)

TED KLAUSTERMAN — Early 30's. From the Midwest. Yale Grad School dropout. Attractive. Charming. Ambitious. A leader. Shifts easily between the intellectually profound and the profoundly silly. Quintessential comedy club M.C. who has gone from being afraid of success to craving it. By the end of the play, he has learned to redefine it.

PHIL KUNIN — Late 20's. From New York. Harvard Law School dropout. Jewish macho. Very intense. Extremely volatile. He is constantly finding and losing his sense of humor, making him both likeable and a little frightening. He is just starting out as a stand-up comic and is torn between career and family.

KENNY BREWSTER — Late 20's. A Zen Catholic suicidal conceptual comic. The guilelessness of a child coupled with the inner torment of a religious fanatic. Kenny's comedy is his sole means of communication. Expert at mime, sound effects, and strange voices. Kenny mixes the familiar with the bizarre. Lovable and tragic.

8

3 Guys Naked from the Waist Down

ACT ONE

[MUSIC #1: OVERTURE]

Darkness. TED's voice is heard accompanied by changing projections. *

TED. (*off-stage on mike*) The time: The 1980's!

(PROJECTION, C., *of Nancy Reagan at podium of Republican convention waving at huge videoscreen of Reagan, bordered by other convention shots*)

The world was poised on the brink of nuclear annihilation!

(PROJECTION, C., *of 'war board' map of the world, showing locations of thousands of missiles; on* R., *Reagan with Bonzo; on* L., *Politburo members on reviewing stand*)

Millions of people were hungry, desperate and out of work.

(PROJECTIONS *of Ford, Nixon, and Carter*)

The situation looked hopeless!

(PROJECTION, C., *of Democratic convention photo of Mondale, Hart, and Jackson on podium in gesture of unity; bordered by other Democratic convention shots*)

And very serious!

(PROJECTION *montage of 1984 current events: Marine bombing in Beirut, Grenada invastion, Reagan and Bonzo, toxic dump sites, people living in cars, Reagan and Bonzo, Watt*

---

*This script describes the projections that were used in the original production. If new productions decide to employ the use of projections, the substitution of up-to-date images, places, and events is suggested.

9

with Shot Foot Award, man setting himself on fire before the press, Reagan and Bonzo, unemployment lines, Reagan and Bonzo, Reagan on horse, Reagan's Chesterfield cigarette ad, Reagan and Bush with Dallas cheerleaders, Reagan and Bonzo)

Until one man!

(PROJECTION *of close-up of TED with "Who,me?" expression*)

One very silly man!

(PROJECTION *of same shot, full-length revealing "Who, me?" T-shirt and pants around ankles*)

Burst onto the stage of the Komedy Klub East!

(PROJECTION *of Komedy Klub East logo in* c. *NYC night skyline on* L. *and* R.)

Ladies and gentlemen: TED KLAUSTERMAN!

(*Lights up, and as entrance music plays, TED runs onto the stage of the KOMEDY KLUB EAST, a Manhattan nightspot where comedians do their thing before their "big break." It consists of a piano, a stool, and a stand-up microphone* c. *stage. TED dances a bit, gives a big button for the band, and grabs the microphone.*)

TED. Hi there! How ya doin'? (*He waits for a reply, ad libs his own response. To BAND:*) How's the band doin' tonight? (*To AUDIENCE:*) My name is Ted Klausterman and I'll be your host here this evening at the Komedy Klub East. Yes, the Komedy Club East, the place where you can sit back, relax, and feel good about the fact that you make more money than anyone you will see on stage tonight. Yes, the Komedy Klub East, the place where young comics get up on the stage just so you can turn to the person sitting next to you and say, "Sure, my life sucks, but at least I'm not a stand-up comic." I know what you're thinking. You're saying to yourselves: "Who is this guy, really?" "Who is this 'Ted'?" "And why do I make more money than him?" Well, I grew up in a small town . . . Peat Moss,

Ohio. Fertilizer capital of America. No shit. Y'know, the number one tourist attraction in downtown Peat Moss is the Tomb of the Very First Man to Spread Oxen Flop on the Fields: Peat Moscowitz. They say that guy was a born hero . . . and yet . . . they also say that heroes aren't born, they're made, but I beg to differ. Take Winston Churchill. If he was made, they wouldn't have made him look like a bulldog. Right? They'd have made him look like Errol Flynn. So what do we learn from this? Well, if you look like a hero, be an actor. If you look like a bulldog, be a hero. And if you look like this (*makes funny face*) be a stand-up comic. Let's see (*points to people in the audience:*) Hero. Actor. Bulldog. Stand-up comic. Bulldog. Bulldog. No, I'm just kidding. You look like an audience . . . of bulldogs . . . No, no, not really. Just this one lady over here. Sorry Mom. Where was I? (*steps back to where he was*) Back in Peat Moss, Ohio, when I was a baby, my father took me outside one summer night and lifted me to the stars and said: "Behold the universe, Teddy, never forget that you are a tiny insignificant speck of cosmic dust. You were born. You will live. You will die. Life has no meaning. Nor does death. Now grow up and *be somebody!*" My father had a Ph.D. in Manic Depression. My mother was a born-again atheist who prayed that God didn't exist so she wouldn't go to Hell. As for me, well, I got the Baby Boom Generation Blues. Child of the 60's. Came of age in the 70's. It's like you wanna be a hero and take all the money in the world and redistribute it in alphabetical order, and yet still afford that summer house in the Hamptons. (*He sits at onstage piano and plays.*) [MUSIC #2: PROMISE OF GREATNESS] But it's the 80's now, and all I want to do is well . . . change other people's lives. Of course, I haven't figured out what the hell to do with my own yet. But you know, life is tough, when you're a deep guy. (*sings*)
I HAD THE PROMISE OF GREATNESS
THE FUTURE WAS GONNA BE MINE
SO I WENT TO AN IVY LEAGUE COLLEGE, BOYS
BUT USED DRUGS TO EXPAND MY MIND

WHOA PROMISE OF GREATNESS
BU DAP DAP I'M A HELLUVA GUY
BU DAP BU DAP BUBA DABA DA DOW
THEY GAVE ME A LADDER
I LOOKED AT THE TOP AND SAID "WOW"
I DON'T THINK I WANNA CLIMB

(*spoken*) I just wanted to be up there already, you know what I mean? Hey, some people love to struggle for success. But not your old pal, Ted. (*sings*)

I SHOULD BE STARRING IN VEGAS
THE MOST POPULAR ARTIST ALIVE
SO I SIGNED WITH THE WILLIAM MORRIS BOYS
BUT PREFER TO PLAY THIS DIVE

CUZ I GOT
PROMISE OF GREATNESS
DU DAP DAP I'M A HELLUVA GUY
BU DAP BU DAP BUBA DABA DA DOW
THEY GAVE ME A ROADMAP
I LOOKED AT THE WHEEL
AND SAID "WOW"
I DON'T THINK I WANNA DRIVE

HEY FOLKS WE'VE ALL GOT OUR PROBLEMS
WAITING FOR FATE TO POINT THE WAY
WHEEL OF FORTUNE
SENDS US SPINNING
WHEN I'M WINNING
I RUN AWAY

I GOT THE PROMISE OF GREATNESS
I WAS GONNA BE FAMOUS AND RICH
SO I TRIED TO BE POP
AND CLASSICAL, BOYS
NOW I CAN'T TELL WHICH IS WHICH

STILL I GOT PROMISE OF GREATNESS
BU DAP DAP I'M A HELLUVA GUY
BU DAP BU DAP BUBA DABA DA DOW
THEY GAVE ME A LADDER,
I LOOKED AT THE TOP
THEY GAVE ME A ROADMAP,
I LOOKED AT THE WHEEL
I GOT ME A MIRROR
I LOOKED AT MY FACE
AND SAID "WOW"
AIN'T LIFE A BITCH
AIN'T LIFE A BITCH

AIN'T LIFE A BITCH

(*TED scats to finish:*)
BA DUBA DUBA DU BOP BA DU DOW
BA DUBA DU BADU DOP
BADU DOP BADU DOP
BA DOW

(*spoken*) Thank you. Thank you. Thank you very much. Thank you. No no. This is too much, you're too kind. I love it. What a night. What a crowd. And what a life!

(*At this point, if latecomers are seated, TED should ad lib. Suggestions: Announcing a horse race with the latecomers as horses with names like "Couldn't Get a Cab," "Fight With the Wife," "The Car Was On the Fritz," "Never Had an Orgasm," etc. He can offer to sing the song again. He can tell the latecomers key words like "Born Again Atheist," "Peat Moss, Ohio." He can reenact what they missed in super fast motion. TED should finish his ad lib by repeating "What a night. What a crowd. And what a life!"*)

And before we continue, I think we should all savor this moment: (*pauses, and gestures to freeze the moment*) O.K., now the man—

(*KENNY BREWSTER walks onstage wearing a hooded monk's robe. TED watches KENNY as KENNY puts down his tape recorder, presses the play/record button, stands on a stool and pantomimes putting a noose around his neck. He then hangs himself, dangles for a moment, takes the imaginary noose off, presses the stop button, picks up the tape recorder and leaves.*)

Ladies and gentlemen, Kenny Brewster. A great guy to hang out with. And with Kenny, you never know when he's gonna drop in with some interesting noose—(*hears groans*) Thank you very much. But until that time, we have a man here tonight whose personality has often been compared to the Great Barrier Reef. This is his first appearance at the Komedy Klub East so let's have a big hand for: PHIL KUNIN!

[MUSIC #3: ANGRY GUY/LOVELY DAY]

(*TED claps. PHIL KUNIN enters through the audience and jumps on the stage. He stares angrily at TED until TED leaves. PHIL looks angrily at the audience, looks away, then looks back with a big grin. He sings.*)

PHIL.
I TELL YA
I'M AN ANGRY GUY
SUCH AN ANGRY GUY
SO YA BETTER WATCH YOUR STEP NOW
PEOPLE LOOK AT ME
WONDER HOW CAN HE
ACT LIKE SUCH AN ANGRY GUY
DON'T KNOW WHY
I FEEL SO PISSED OFF AND JERKED AROUND
I'M AN ANGRY GUY
(*spoken*) Yeah, I gotta tell ya, sometimes New York City really gets to me. I know that in New York City, I cannot get from here to there without running into someone who is determined to just rub my fur the wrong way. Yeah, I'm an angry guy. (*smiles*) But sometimes I wake up in the morning and the hot water's working and the birds are chirping, and I think to myself: (*sings*)
WHAT A LOVELY DAY
AS I LOOK OUT MY WINDOW
I THINK MAYBE SOMEHOW
EVERYTHING'S O.K.
(*spoken*) So I open the door to my apartment and pick up the newspaper. (*Reads headline:*) DEAD MOM GIVES BIRTH IN COFFIN! (*Opens newspaper:*) DOG BLOWS UP IN TANNING SALON! This is information I really need. O.K. So I walk outside, take a deep breath and look at all those busy people. They're good people. I like them. It's O.K. But wait a minute. Look at this. Some guy standing right in front of me just lets his dog take a crap on the sidewalk and then he walks away. I said, "Excuse me, sir, but you can't leave that there." The guy turns around and he goes, "Oh yeah?" (*points to his privates*) Right here, pal." O.K. Well I guess I didn't have much choice, so I pulled out my baseball bat and (*makes smashing sound*) shattered both his kneecaps. (*sings*)
CUZ I'M AN ANGRY GUY

YEAH AN ANGRY GUY
EVERYBODY WATCH YOUR STEP—
(*spoken*) You wanna know a great way to screw up a guy's sex life? Just mess up those kneecaps. Any of you guys ever try to make love to a woman when you can't put any pressure on your knees? Unless you've got a pool table, you're shit out of luck. (*sings*)
EVERYWHERE I GO
PEOPLE OUGHTA KNOW
THAT I'M JUST AN ANGRY GUY
DON'T KNOW WHY
(*spoken*) So I went to the corner and I put my baseball bat in a trashcan. I didn't want any more trouble. (*sings*)
CUZ IT'S A LOVELY DAY
(*spoken*) O.K. So I headed off to the reservoir to meet my girlfriend. Everybody's gotta have a—

(*KENNY staggers across as St. Sebastian, covered with arrows. PHIL gets upset, doesn't know what to do.*)

PHIL. (*Cont'd. To KENNY:*) What're you doin' man? I'm right in the middle of—(*KENNY presses the stop button on his tape recorder and stumbles off. To audience:*) Oh shit. Where was I?

(*PHIL waits for someone in the audience to remind him. If no one responds, PHIL says:*) Nobody knows? (*Waits again. When someone helps him out, he says:*) Right. Thanks.)

O.K. I'm going to the reservoir to meet my girlfriend. All right, so I thought to myself: Go. Get on a bus. You'll get there. You'll be fine. No hassle. Right? O.K. So a bus comes. I get on the bus. The bus is packed. So I inch my way to the back. (*does exaggerated dance to the back of the bus*) And there, sitting in the back seat, is a young man with a fifty pound stereo box with the volume up to full blast. (*imitates a rap song, a capella:*)
YOU A CHUMP, MOTHERFUCKER
  BOOM BOOM THAT'S RIGHT
YOU A JIVE MOTHERFUCKER
  BOOM BOOM YOU CHUMP
YOU CHUMP BOOM JIVE BOOM
  CHUMP JIVE MOTHERFUCKER

YEAH BOOM BOOM

We've got a big communication problem in this country. How am I to communicate to this young man that he should turn his music down? Wait a minute, I know, it just came to me. I'll ask him politely. "Excuse me, listen, could you please turn the music down?!" Kid looks at me and he goes (*Takes deep toke on a joint and mouths:* "Fuck you, motherfucker.") O.K., so I snatch the stereo out of his hands, I push open the emergency window, and I throw the goddamn machine out into the street. The entire bus bursts into applause. I take it in for a few minutes and then I tell 'em all to *shut the fuck up*!! (*sings*)

CUZ I'M AN ANGRY GUY
YEAH THE KIND OF GUY
FOLKS DON'T LIKE TO RIDE ON A BUS WITH
(*spoken*) So I get off the bus and cross the street to get to the park. (*sings*)
CUZ IT'S A LOVELY DAY
COULD IT BE THAT I'M OVERREACTING
PLEASE SOMEONE TELL ME EVERYTHING'S O.K.
(*spoken*) So there I am . . . crossing the street, looking for my girlfriend . . . the sign says WALK (*pronounced "WAHLLK"*), in big white letters . . . So I'm walking (*"wahllkeeng"*) . . . and then suddenly— RRRRRRRRRRRRRRRRRP! (*MUSIC out.*) This old geezer in a Datsun rips 'round the corner and almost runs me down. O.K. So I run after him for about ten blocks, and I'm just about to catch him when I slipped on a pile of dogshit, smashed into a tree and *shattered both my kneecaps!* (*MUSIC up. He sings:*)

I'M AN ANGRY GUY
ON A LOVELY DAY
EVERYBODY WATCH YOUR STEP NOW
HAD TO KICK THE TREE
FOR MESSING UP MY KNEES
SCREAMING LIKE A CRAZY GUY
I SEE MY GIRL
AND SHE SAYS "LET'S TAKE A WALK AND GREET
     ALL THE FRIENDLY
     PEOPLE OUT ON THE STREET
     IT'S A LOVELY—"
I SAID, "LOOK AT MY KNEES
     I'M AN ANGRY—"
SHE SAID, "GIVE ME A SQUEEZE,
     YOU'RE A LOVELY—"

I SAID "DON'T START TO TEASE
   I'M AN ANGRY DAY—
   NO, I'M A LOVELY GUY—
   NO, IT'S AN ANGRY GUY—
   NO, I'M A LOVELY DAY—
   NO, I'M AN ANGRY GUY
   ON A LOVELY DAY"

(*spoken*) This really happened to me. I had to go out and buy a used pool table. I gotta tell ya, it really pissed me off too. You know why? Because that old geezer in the Datsun almost killed me just so he could get to the next red light. What, maybe a few seconds faster? I mean. This is great. I love the mentality. Save two seconds, kill a pedestrian. What is this? I mean, maybe, maybe if I hadn't quit law school, (*moves away from microphone*) I could've taken that guy in the car to court and sued his ass. Right? God knows I need the money. I mean, I'm still paying off my student loans. And I'm just getting started here on my career. And my girlfriend, she wants to have a baby and I cannot walk across the goddamn street without *some asshole trying to kill me! Now what's going on?* I mean, are we supposed to pretend that we don't care about these things? Are we supposed to pretend that human life is so easily expendable? I mean why do so many people act as if *nobody else* counts for anything any more, huh? AND WHY DO WE LET THESE PEOPLE WALK AROUND WITH THIS BULLSHIT ATTITUDE WITHOUT SMASHING THEIR FUCKING FACES IN?!!

(*KENNY enters be-headed with a dummy head in his hands. PHIL hears laughter, doesn't know why, turns around, sees KENNY.*)

What're you doin'? I'm not finished!

(*TED enters through the audience and pauses at the edge of the stage.*
KENNY puts his cassette down, places the head on top of the piano, and picks up the cassette. TED comes on stage. PHIL sees him, then looks back at KENNY who presses the 'stop' button. PHIL storms off. KENNY stumbles off.)

TED. There goes an angry guy. (*Gestures to where KENNY*

exited:) And you've just met the third member of the Kenny Brewster Hall of Martyrs. As you can see, *Comedy Is Dangerous.* But you can relax now that I'm here. (*opens shirt revealing "Who, me?" T-shirt*) Anybody in the audience dying to get a head? Ooh. You're right. You're right. But is there anybody here who is right all the time? Just raise your hands. Don't be shy. I used to be right all the time. When I was two. Then at age three, I kissed the toaster . . . Why? . . . Well, I was admiring my reflection. My lips would still be on that toaster today if my Dad hadn't been there with a handful of ice. (*crosses to piano*) He said, "Teddy, don't be an asshole. The world is a hot toaster, son. So don't kiss it. Make toast." Y'know, life is tough when you've got a deep Dad.

[MUSIC #4: PROMISE OF GREATNESS — REPRISE]

(*sings*)
I GOT THE PROMISE OF GREATNESS
POSTERITY CALLING MY NAME
SO I DREAM OF SUCCESS AND FAILURE, BOYS,
AND HOPE THEY'RE NOT THE SAME

CUZ I GOT
THE PROMISE OF GREATNESS
DU DAP DAP
I'M A HELLUVA GUY
BU DAP BU DAP BUBA DABA DA DOW
I PUT DOWN MY MARKER
I RATTLED THE DICE
AND SAID "WOW"
(*spoken*) I don't want to play this game. I'd rather play 'Kiss the Toaster.' (*sings*)
CUZ AIN'T LIFE A BITCH! AIN'T LIFE A BITCH!
(*spoken*) Everybody! (*sings*)
AIN'T LIFE A BITCH!
(*spoken*) Goodnight. Thanks for coming.

(*The Komedy Klub East set, with TED still at the piano, rolls back, disappearing through the ribbon curtain.*
PROJECTIONS *of the street and back alley of the club. PHIL comes on the bare stage, working out his frustrations by bouncing a basketball, on his way home. TED enters, beer in hand, the very picture of affability.*

The following goes in and out of regular conversation and rhythmic patter. The patter is in CAPITAL LETTERS and is rhythmically punctuated by PHIL and TED with bounces and tosses of the basketball.)

TED. How ya doin'?

PHIL. What?

TED. How's it goin'?

PHIL. All right.

TED. All right. Listen, you were good tonight.

PHIL. Thanks. (*PHIL starts to leave.*)

TED. You really quit law school, huh?

PHIL. Yeah.

TED. Yeah. Well, I went for a Masters in Philosophy. I figured there was good money in pondering the universe. I pondered wrong, so I left. Why'd you leave, man? I mean, a good lawyer's set for life.

PHIL. Yeah. Right. Set for life. Look, I just left, O.K.?

TED. O.K. And now you're a comic.

PHIL. I'm just starting out, all right?

TED. Yeah, well, you've got a long way to go if you think you can lose it in front of an audience, pal. (*starts to leave*)

PHIL. Hey look, I just wanted to make a point.

TED. (*comes back*) All right, but if you wanna make a point you've got to be in control. They don't wanna be preached to. You get 'em laughing, you have fun, *then* you slip your point in, and if they're still laughing, that's when you're cookin'.

PHIL. Yeah, I know the feeling. Look man, back at school I used to hit this bar around midnight. I'd get up on top of a table and take potshots at everything from the legal profession to government studies studying the cost of government studies. I gotta tell ya man, in the classroom, I didn't have a damn thing to say, and maybe not in a courtroom . . . but you put me in a place where the booze is flowin' and you throw away the goddamn rulebook, and people would listen to me, man. I was a goddamn star.

TED. Yeah, a star of college bars.

PHIL. It was a beginning. And you wanna be a star M.C.

TED. It's a beginning. Actually, it's beginning to hold me back. Once you get known as an M.C., it's hard to get anything beyond the clubs. So I'm looking for a fresher approach, y'know? A new tack. (*laughs to himself*) You need instant experience and I need — wait a minute. Wait a minute. You're an angry guy, I'm a helluva guy. What a team, huh? Maybe we can work together.

PHIL. Oh no, I've got enough people to worry about now.

TED. Whaddya mean?

PHIL. My girlfriend's pregnant.

TED. Congratulations.

PHIL. Hey, I'm not ready to have a baby. I can't even take care of myself. I can't even handle it when some asshole comes across the stage in the middle of my routine.

TED. That's why you need me. I handle assholes.

PHIL. Who the hell was that guy?

TED. Kenny Brewster.

PHIL. All right, you tell him if he pulls that shit on me again, I'm gonna get my baseball bat and . . . (*shoves basketball into TED's gut*) shatter his sex life.

TED. Kenny has no sex life, he's a Zen Catholic.

PHIL. What's a Zen Catholic?

TED. Nobody knows. And Kenny isn't talking.

PHIL. He's weird.

TED. He's my best friend.

PHIL. Why don't you work with him?

TED. I asked him to about a year ago.

PHIL. And?

TED. He hasn't answered me yet.

PHIL. O.K., I'll get back to you in a year.

TED. All right. Look, you wanna get ahead in this business? Let me tell you about Paris.

PHIL. France?

TED.

NO, RICK (*bounces ball*) PARIS.

PHIL.

HE'S IN FRANCE?

TED.

THAT'S ONE FOR YOU. NOW RICK (*bounce*) PARIS IS A BUDDY OF MINE FROM YALE.

PHIL.

OH, A BUDDY OF YOURS FROM YALE

TED.

THAT'S RIGHT, AND RICK (*bounce*) PARIS JUST BECAME HEAD TALENT SCOUT FOR JOHNNY CARSON

PHIL.

WAIT . . . JOHNNY CARSON?

TED.
JOHNNY CARSON
    PHIL.
OH WOW
    TED.
AND HOW
    PHIL.
NO SHIT
    TED.
YOU WILL — And listen. Paris is looking for a comedy team. Now can you picture yourself on Carson? All you need is the connections. I got 'em. You work with me, and as soon as we're ready, I'll have Paris come and take a look at us.

    PHIL. You and me on Carson, huh?

    TED. You got it. And I'll tell you what . . . the first thing we do together . . . is break into the middle of Brewster's routine.

[MUSIC #4A: RAP #1]

    PHIL. (*smiles*)
SOUNDS GOOD (*bounce*)
    TED.
SOUNDS FUN (*bounce*)
    PHIL.
IT'S A KICK (*bounce*)
    TED.
IT'S A RUSH (*bounce*)
    PHIL.
AND WE'LL GET 'EM ALL TO LAUGH
    TED.
AND WE'LL GET 'EM ALL TO LISTEN
AND WE'LL SCORE A COUPLE POINTS
    PHIL.
YEAH, I NEED A COUPLE POINTS
    TED.
OH YEAH!
AND IF WE DO IT RIGHT
BEFORE YOU KNOW IT WE'LL BE ON CARSON
    PHIL.
ON CARSON?

(PROJECTION *of NYC night skyline*)

TED.

WHY NOT?

(*The "LAST STAND UP" set starts rolling on.*)

AND IF WE PULL OUR SHIT TOGETHER

AND WE WATCH OUR FUCKING LANGUAGE

AND WE MAKE OUR CRAP ACCESSIBLE

THE NEXT THING YOU KNOW WE'LL BE SUPERSTARS

PHIL.

SUPERSTARS?

TED.

SUPER—

PHIL.

SUPERSTAR?

TED.

STAR—

TED & PHIL.

YEAH!

PHIL.

I DON'T WANNA BE A SUPERSTAR . . .

TED.

YOU DON'T WANNA BE A SUPERSTAR?!!

[MUSIC #5: SUPERSTAR I]

(*Spotlight on PHIL and TED, now on the stage of the LAST STAND UP, another popular comedy nightclub, complete with piano, mike, and three stools. Above, a* PROJECTION *of 'THE LAST STAND UP' logo, flanked by New York City nightlights. The Band starts playing. Without skipping a beat, PHIL and TED jump into performance.*)

PHIL.

DON'T WANNA BE NO SUPERSTAR

DON'T WANNA DRIVE NO FANCY CAR

DON'T LIKE THE SMELL OF CAVIAR

TED.

JUST WANNA WORK ON THE FAMILY FARM

PHIL.

DON'T WANNA HAVETA FLY FIRST CLASS

TED.

DON'T WANT ATTENTION WHEN I PASS

PHIL.
DON'T WANT MY HEART TO BEAT TOO FAST
OH NO
TED.
OH NO
PHIL.
I DON'T
TED.
I DON'T
TED & PHIL.
WANNA BE A SUPERSTAR

TED.
LET SOMEBODY ELSE SPARKLE
PHIL.
LET SOMEBODY ELSE SHINE
TED.
WHEN I HEAR ABOUT THEIR PROBLEMS
PHIL.
I'LL BE HAPPY THAT THEY'RE NOT MINE

TED & PHIL.
DON'T WANNA DINE WITH FAMOUS FOLK
DON'T WANNA SNORT NO L.A. COKE
DON'T WANNA BIG FUSS WHEN I CROAK
PHIL.
OH NO
TED.
OH NO
PHIL.
I DON'T
TED.
I DON'T
TED & PHIL.
WANNA BE A SUPERSTAR
WANNA BE A SUPERSTAR
OH NO DON'T WANNA BE A SUPERSTAR

(*PHIL leaves.*)

TED. O.K. Ladies and gentlemen, welcome to the Last Stand-

Up, the place where you can sit back, relax, and watch young comics get up on stage and do things they've never done before. So to put us in the right mood, let's *all* do something we've never done before. O.K.? On three. Ready? One. Two. (*TED turns away.*) Three. (*TED turns back.*) What'd you do? No, it's all right. I won't tell. I just wanted to—Didn't give you enough time, did I? Time's funny. It doesn't really exist. We just pretend it does so we know when to do things. Actually, space doesn't exist either, until you put something around it. But wait a minute . . . matter itself doesn't exist without time or space. Oh my God! Oh no, *we're not here*!! Well, now that we know this . . . let's all have sex. Whaddya say? (*To member of audience:*) Sir! I was just kidding. It's a metaphysical joke. You can't—

(*KENNY has come on with his dummy, STEVE. TED exits.*)

STEVE. (*to KENNY*) Listen, I told you a hundred times. Just go out there and do it. Don't worry about feelin' right. Yer never gonna "feel right." You just need somebody to keep an eye on ya. Stick me over there. (*KENNY hangs STEVE on microphone stand* US.) I'll watch ya. Good. Now get out there and do it!

(*KENNY walks cautiously to* C. *stage. Large sheet wrapped around head and body. [See "Director's notes"]*)

KENNY. I think it was a good idea that I came here today. (*He makes sweet bird chirping noises. He sees the bird, reaches for it. He does machine gun fire, and watches bird drop dead.*) I rode on the bus today but the driver got mad and made me get back inside. (*He does pigeon noises, looks in other direction, does bomb dropping on it.*) So I took the express train instead but the conductor made me put it back. (*He does sound of baby chicks, looks around for source of sound. With back to audience, he does long screamer sound of bomb dropping. It explodes. KENNY's whole body vibrates. He turns around, arms spread like airplane. Making airplane sounds:*) Detroit! (*drops bomb*) Rhodesia! (*drops bomb; African voice, head covering:*) "No. Zimbabwe!" (*Dartgun; Englishman caught in neck:*) "Good shot. But you know you can't win." (*Russian cape:*) "Ve vill be victorious. Have secret plan. Bomb Disneyland. Goodbye Goofy." (*LITTLE KID sings 'IT'S A SMALL WORLD AFTER ALL . . .' then reacts to atom bomb. Covers himself with a sheet as if it were a child's tent. LITTLE KID:*) Hey come on in here. The president says it'll be safe. (*OTHER KID:*) Hey Pinhead, can I come in? (*FIRST KID:*) Yeah sure, did you bring the Cheese Puffs? (*SECOND KID:*) No, but I brought a couple of friends. (*THIRD KID:*) Hey, what a neat space. (*ANOTHER KID:*) I like the swimming pool. Oh, hi Flipper. (*Flipper noises. FOURTH KID:*) Can I use the ping pong table? (*FIRST KID:*) Sure, if you brought your own balls. (*He does ping pong match. SECOND KID:*) Hey somebody get Dumbo off the ping pong table. (*Elephant call. KID:*) Don't tell me what to do. (*THIRD KID:*) I will if I want to. (*SECOND KID:*) Oh yeah! (*FIRST KID: Screams. Ripping sound. Severed hand falls out from under sheet. THIRD KID:*) Ow! You asked for it, Jerkface! (*Scream. Ripping sound. Severed foot falls out from sheet. SECOND KID:*) Great, how am I gonna explain this to Mom? (*THIRD KID:*) Shut-up. (*Screams. Ripping sound. Severed arm falls out. SECOND KID:*) Thanks a lot. Now I can't finish the ping pong game. (*FIRST KID:*) Use your stump as a paddle. (*Phone rings; pulls phone out and emerges from sheet.*) Hello? Hello? [MUSIC #6: OPERATOR PART I] (*KENNY sings.*)

OPERATOR
OPERATOR
PLEASE STAY ON THE LINE
I'VE GOT NO ONE TO TALK TO
I'M RUNNING OUT OF TIME

THE RAZOR'S COMING, COMING CLOSER
AND I'M FILLING UP THE TUB
I CUT MY RUBBER DUCK
I'M GONNA SHAVE MY LEGS

OOH OOH OPERATOR
HEADSET'S ON YOUR EARS
MOUTHPIECE NEAR YOUR CHIN
OOH OOH OPERATOR
GARTER BELT'S ROUND YOUR HIPS
LIPSTICK ON YOUR LIPS

Hello? (*mumble*) Who is this? (*mumble*) Look, we've already seen him and we don't think he's right for the part. No! No! Don't send him over! (*Does King Kong. Climbs Empire State Building. Japanese:*) Aw shit! We gotta stop that monkey! Send for Bluce Ree! (*Does Bruce Lee Kung Fu poses and yipping sounds. Does spin-around kick, becomes King Kong and bops Bruce Lee on the head. Japanese:*) Aw shit, We in big tlouble! King Kong is destroying the Big Apple! (*Bites the apple. Chokes. Spits it out.*) Oh no! Sister Perpetua! I coughed up a piece of my lung. What do I do? What do I do? (*mouthless picture*) That's very good, Kenneth. Don't forget, it requires lots of sunlight and water so its roots can take firm hold. (*disbelief:*) She wants me to plant my lung! Blech! A cat throwing up: (*Does cat throwing up.*) A cat having sex! (*Does cat having sex.*) A cat who hates sex: (*Mixes the two. Sees little stuffed cat.*) I'm sorry, I didn't mean it. (*Pets the cat. Makes heartbeat sound. Cat attacks him, knocking him to the ground. KENNY fights back and chokes it to death. LITTLE BOY:*) He's dead. You killed him. (*BRANDO:*) The horror. The horror. Sonny's dead. Michael's jaw is busted and some bum killed my kitty kat. (*FAITH HEALER:*) Stand back. I'll save him. 'Praise the Lord,' and rise! (*He smacks it:*) Praise the Lord and rise! (*smacks it again:*) Cut to a commercial! (*grabs phone*) Help! Whaddya mean hang up the phone and dial again? You think I wanna go through life making the same mistake twice? I'm talking to a machine. (*HAL:*) Don't worry Dave. I'm not going to hurt you. (*KIRK:*) Scotty, beam me outa here. (*SCOTTY:*) I can't captain. The dilithium crystals are fading fast. She's going to blow! (*Close Encounters music*) 500,000 years in the same spaceship as Richard Dreyfus! No! No! (*Star Wars laser gun. YODA:*) You must spend time with Dreyfus to become Jedi warrior. (*LORRE:*) Maybe if we inject him with some automatic transmission fluid. (*Injects cat. It flies away.*) EEEEE! (*Turns needle on himself.*) Hey. George what're you doin' with that needle, George? (*GEORGE from "Of Mice and Men":*) This is it Lenny. I'm sick and tired of telling you about those goddamn rabbits. (*LENNY:*) I won't ask you about the rabbits George. I won't George, honest I won't. (*GEORGE:*) All right, Lenny. I'm sorry. I don't know what came over me. (*LENNY:*) George, tell me about the rabbits. (*GEORGE:*) That's it! (*LENNY:*) Don't do it! (*GEORGE:*) Too late! (*Plunges needle into his arm. WICKED WITCH:*) Aah, I'm melting, melting. What a world, what a world, who would think such an innocent girl like you could destroy such a beautiful dream like mine. Aah. (*MICKEY MOUSE hat and bullwhip.*) Shay, Kidsh! Ya wanna have a great time?! (*KID:*) Yeah, yeah, I wanna have a great time. (*Rasping voice:*) C'mere. Pull down your pants and bend over! (*Cracks the whip.*) What have I done? Oh my God, I killed him. He never did anything to me. I must be punished. [MUSIC #6: OPERATOR PART II] (*presses the button on cassette recorder*)

TAPE. (*or offstage voice*)
OPERATOR, OPERATOR, OPERATOR
GRANT ME THIS ONE
GRANT ME THIS ONE THING
OPERATOR, OPERATOR, OPERATOR, OPERATOR
OPERATOR, OPERATOR,

OPERATOR,
OPERATOR
WHEN YOU'RE
FLOATING UNDER-
  GROUND
FLOATING
UNDERGROUND
FLOATING
UNDERGROUND . . .

OPERATOR,
OPERATOR
OPERATOR,
OPERATOR
AS I
DROWN . . .

KENNY.
THE SEWER LOOKS
SO ATTRACTIVE
WHEN YOU'RE
FLOATING
UNDERGROUND

YOU'VE GOT
TO HOLD ON
TO ME
SEND WAVES OF PASSION
THROUGH ME
ATTACH YOURSELF
ONTO ME
AS I DROWN . . .

(*Tape voice crescendos, stops.*)

KENNY.
OOH OOH OPERATOR
HEADSET'S ON YOUR EARS
MOUTHPIECE NEAR YOUR CHIN
OOH OOH OPERATOR
GARTER BELT'S ROUND YOUR HIPS
LIPSTICK ON YOUR LIPS
(*whispers*) I'm hanging up now . . .
OOH OOH OOH
OOH OOH OOH

(*KENNY gathers his props together like a child would gather his toys. He hugs them to his body as the lights fade. In the dark, KENNY picks up his dummy, STEVE, sits on stool. Lights up.*)

STEVE. Hey c'mere, lemme ask you something. You got some kinda problem with the telephone?

KENNY. No, Steve, I—

STEVE. Shuddup. Listen, there's somethin' wrong with you. I mean, those noises you were making were funny, but why would you wanna go and shave your legs?

KENNY. I already did.

STEVE. What?!

KENNY. Yeah, I shaved them.

(*As KENNY and STEVE bend over to check KENNY's leg, PHIL, head lowered, a strip of blue tape across his mouth, enters with his dummy, SPIKE. They sit on 2nd stool. His hand is covering SPIKE's face. PHIL looks up revealing the tape on his mouth. He takes his hand away, revealing a piece of blue tape on SPIKE's mouth. He rips the tape from his own mouth, then rips the tape from SPIKE's.*)

SPIKE. *Ow!* What'd you do that for, Kunin?

PHIL. I felt like it, Spike. You piss me off.

SPIKE. Yeah, everything pisses you off. You're always complainin'. Why don't you go and make the world a better place to live?

PHIL. Yeah? How should I do that?

SPIKE. Go live somewhere else. Ha Ha Ha.

PHIL. Oh, that's very funny. (*smashes beer can on SPIKE's head*)

STEVE. (*to KENNY*) Let's get outa here, the neighborhood's changing.

KENNY. Yeah.

PHIL. (*to KENNY and STEVE*) *Wait a minute!* (*to TED*) Oh, Mr. Dirtball!

(*TED enters with his dummy, MR. DIRTBALL and sits on 3rd stool.*)

MR. DIRTBALL. Hey Phil, hey Spike. Steve! How ya doin'?

STEVE. Mr. Dirtball? Spike? Who are these guys?

SPIKE. We're a singing group.

MR. DIRTBALL. A 5, 6, 7, 8—

[MUSIC #7: DUMMIES]

TED. (*sings*)
I GOT THE PROMISE OF GREATNESS
    SPIKE & MR. DIRTBALL.
GREATNESS
    TED.
SUCCESS WILL BE WAITING FOR ME
WHEN I FIND THE RIGHT KIND OF VOICES TO
JOIN IN HARMONY
    SPIKE & MR. DIRTBALL.
BE DOP BE DOP
    STEVE. That's great. Let's blow. (*KENNY & STEVE start to leave.*)
    TED. Wait a second Steve. We thought you might sing with us.
    STEVE. Gee that's tough, cuz I don't sing back-up.
    PHIL. (*to SPIKE*) Oh you hear that? He thinks he's too good to sing back-up.
    SPIKE. Yeah, let's get out of here before the other guy starts to sing to the telephone again. (*PHIL & SPIKE start to leave.*)
    STEVE. Yeah, good idea, and don't forget to put the tape back on both your big fat mouths. (*laughs*)
    TED. Hey, c'mon, Steve, Spike, let's all try to be friends here. O.K.?
    MR. DIRTBALL. Friends?! You don't wanna be friends with those guys. They're bad news, man. They're just gonna pull ya down.
    STEVE. Oh yeah?!
    MR. DIRTBALL. Yeah!
    SPIKE. Oh yeah! Look who's talkin'. Just another Ivy League nobody.
    STEVE. Yeah, why don't you go back to pondering the universe, pal.
    TED. Look, guys, he didn't mean it.
    MR. DIRTBALL. You bet your ass I meant it.
    PHIL. Hey, maybe you better tell your little friend to shut-up.
    KENNY. Yeah.
    SPIKE. Yeah! (*to PHIL*) Wait! You Shut-up! You're the one who's always looking for trouble.
    STEVE. Yeah, you shut-up too, Brewster, yer getting on my nerves.
    TED. Look guys—
    MR. DIRTBALL. (*to TED*) Shut-up! Cuz you're the one who started the whole thing.
    SPIKE. No, Kunin started it.

STEVE. (*to KENNY*) No, Brewster started it.

MR. DIRTBALL. No, Klausterman started it. (*They all argue with their DUMMIES.*)

TED, PHIL & KENNY. (*to their DUMMIES*) SHHHHHHHHH!

(*"THE LAST STAND UP" logo* PROJECTION *fades out, as the Comedy Club rolls back through the ribbon curtain and disappears, leaving TED, PHIL, and KENNY on their three stools. MUSIC vamps.*)

TED. (*sings*)
HEY CATS,
THE CLOCKS ARE SCREAMING IN THE NIGHT

STEVE. What's he talkin' about?

TED.
HEY CATS,
LISTEN TIGHT FOR THE NEXT URBAN EXPLOSION

SPIKE.
Who are these guys?

TED.
A voice.

STEVE.
Yeah?

PHIL.
Two voices.

MR. DIRTBALL.
Wow.

KENNY.
Three voices.

SPIKE.
Right.

TED.
AND A VISION

PHIL.
OF THE POSSIBLE

KENNY.
IN A BACKWARD TIME OF SCREAMING CLOCKS

SPIKE.
What're they on?

MR. DIRTBALL.
What're they on?

PHIL.

ON SUPER VICIOUS CYCLE BREAKING VISTAS

STEVE.

Speak English.

TED.

O.K., I'm gonna lay it on you lightly.

DUMMIES.

Ready!

TED.

WE HAD A BABY BOOM AFTER WORLD WAR II

PHIL. (*joking*)

He loves to spew.

SPIKE.

So do you.

TED.

WITH AMERICA ON TOP OF THE HEAP

KENNY.

WITH STEEL

PHIL.

POWER

TED.

MONEY

KENNY.

FEAR

SPIKE.

Fear?!

TED.

Hey, but what's happening here?

PHIL.

THEY'RE ASKING QUESTIONS IN THE COFFEE CLUBS

KENNY.

IN THE MUSIC AND THE MANNERS OF A DIFFERENT

TED.

SUB

PHIL.

STRATA

TED, PHIL, & KENNY.

UNDERGROUND

TED.

WAITING TO EMERGE

TED, PHIL & KENNY.

FROM THE FIFTIES SIXTIES HIPPIES AND
THE BLOOD AND THE FLOOD OF REVOLUTION

FROM THE NO WIN WAR TO BETRAYAL OF TRUST
TO A CYNICAL TIME TURNING IN TO
  MR. DIRTBALL.
Me!
  SPIKE.
Me!
  STEVE.
Me!
  DUMMIES.
Yeah, the Me Generation!
  TED.
WITH THE BABY BOOM BOOMERS AND THE
WORLD WAR II SURVIVORS SAYING
  PHIL.
Climb the heap.
  KENNY.
Step on the heap.
  TED.
WE'RE GOING BACK IN TIME
  KENNY. To simple answers.
  SPIKE. Get a job!
  MR. DIRTBALL. Balance the budget!
  STEVE. A nuclear war is winnable. (*MUSIC out.*)
  MR. DIRTBALL. Possible.
  SPIKE. Plannable.
  TED. (*Reagan*) But don't worry Bonzo. We'll be on the ranch.
  TED, PHIL & KENNY. (*MUSIC up.*)
BUT THE STATUS QUO IS CLAMPING TIGHT
AND THE VOICES STILL SCREAM IN THE NIGHT.
  SPIKE.
What are they screaming for?
  TED.
FOR A NEWER VOICE TO SPEAK
  STEVE.
Yeah? Who you got in mind?
  PHIL.
AND IT AIN'T THE KIDS IN VIDEO BLISS
  KENNY.
AND IT AIN'T THE ESTABLISHMENT

(*TED, PHIL and KENNY look at DUMMIES, DUMMIES look
   at them, DUMMIES look at each other.*)

Dummies.

Ahhhhhhhhhh!

Ted.

AND THE ONES WHO REMAIN ARE US

Steve.

We hear ya.

Phil.

WE GOTTA MAKE OUTRAGE CONTAGIOUS

Mr. Dirtball.

You better believe it.

Kenny.

EVERYBODY WATCH ME NOW

HEAR ME NOW

Ted, Phil & Kenny.

SEE WITHOUT SIGHT

HEAR WITHOUT SOUND

Dummies.

Sing it!

Ted, Phil & Kenny.

WE'RE THE NEXT GENERATION OF HEROES

Mr. Dirtball.

Now you're talkin'!

Ted, Phil & Kenny.

WE'RE THE NEXT REVOLUTION OF

THOUGHT-ACTION-DEED

Ted.

ARE WE READY TO BLEED?

Phil & Kenny.

WHOA YEAH!

(*TED, PHIL and KENNY leave their stools and move* DS. *with their DUMMIES.*)

Ted, Phil & Kenny.

POISED TO BLEED, GIVE US A CHANCE

BLEED FOR TRUTH, WORTH STANDING UP FOR

LIFE AND DEATH, WEALTH AND WASTE

SHOUTING OUT, THOSE CLOCKS SCREAM IN THE

   NIGHT

STATUS QUO, BABY BOOM

INDUSTRIAL AGE OF GREED AND ENVY
THERE'S PEOPLE OUT THERE
TRAMPLED ON
SWALLOWED UP BY COMPLACENT FRUSTRATION
AND THE ONLY CHANCE
FOR A BETTER CHANCE
IS TO PULL OUT SOMETHING UNEXPECTED,
UNAFFECTED,
UNSUSPECTED
POP A FEW EYES
TICKLE SOME MINDS
PULL DOWN YOUR PANTS AND BARE YOUR BEHINDS
(*They drop the DUMMIES' trousers.*)
　STEVE.
HEY CATS,
THE CLOCKS ARE SCREAMING
　SPIKE.
SCREAMING
　MR. DIRTBALL.
SCREAMING
　TED, PHIL & KENNY.
YEAH!

(*BLACKOUT*)

[MUSIC #7A: DUMMIES PLAYOFF]

(*Lights up.* PROJECTIONS *of NYC night lights. During the following,* TED, PHIL, *and* KENNY *make their way up one stairway, across the band platform, and down the other stairway.*)

PHIL. Look, Ted, Ted! I know you wrote this thing, but—you really think Rick Paris is gonna like this?
TED. He'll love it.
PHIL. I don't know, man.
KENNY. I don't know, man.
TED. Kenny, help me out on this, all right? Look Phil, Paris said he wanted something like the Marx Brothers or the Ritz brothers.
KENNY. The Ritz Brothers.

PHIL. Then why are we doing a history song like Gilbert and Sullivan?

KENNY. Gilbert and Sullivan.

PHIL. Is there something wrong with him?

TED. No no, he's fine. (*to KENNY*) You all right?

KENNY. T's'all right.

TED. Look Phil, Paris was a history major at Yale, and he was a Gilbert and Sullivan nut!

PHIL. Terrific. But I'm not gonna wear that costume.

TED. Look. Wear the costume. Y'know I wish you guys would just trust me for once. Every time we—

[MUSIC #7B: RAP #2]

(*in rhythm*)

HE'LL EAT IT UP.

KENNY. (*picking it up*)

HE'LL EAT IT UP.

(*Set starts to roll on.*)

PHIL.

IF WE DO IT RIGHT

TED.

WE'LL DO IT RIGHT

PHIL.

WE'LL EAT IT

TED.

WE'LL DO IT

KENNY.

WL'LL EAT IT

PHIL.

WE'LL BITE IT

TED.

HE'LL LOVE IT

PHIL.

HE'LL LOVE IT?

TED.

LET'S DO IT

TED. (*excited*) & PHIL. (*resigned*)

ALL RIGHT! YEAH!

TED.

AND IF WE PULL OUR SHIT TOGETHER

PHIL.

AND WE WATCH OUR FUCKING LANGUAGE

TED.
AND WE MAKE OUR CRAP ACCESSIBLE
THE NEXT THING YOU KNOW WE'LL BE SUPERSTARS
    KENNY.
SUPERSTARS?
    PHIL.
SUPER!
    TED.
SUPERSTAR!
    KENNY.
STAR?
    TED & PHIL.
YEAH!
    KENNY.
I DON'T WANNA BE A SUPERSTAR!
    TED & PHIL.
YOU DON'T WANNA BE A SUPERSTAR?

[MUSIC #8: SUPERSTAR II]

(*Lights change. MUSIC up. They are on the stage of THE
    FUNNY FARM, another New York comedy nightclub.
    Above, a* PROJECTION *of "THE FUNNY FARM" logo.
    Perfectly in synch, all three are in mid-performance.*)

    TED, PHIL & KENNY. (*sing*)
DON'T WANNA BE NO SUPERSTAR
DON'T WANNA BE TOO POPULAR
DON'T WANNA BE LOVED FROM AFAR.
    KENNY.
OH NO
    TED & PHIL.
OH NO
    KENNY.
I DON'T
    TED & PHIL.
I DON'T
    KENNY, PHIL, TED.
WANNA BE A SUPER
SUPERSTAR
OH NO
DON'T WANNA BE
NO!

OH NO!
I DON'T
WANNA BE A SUPERSTAR

[MUSIC #8A: ARKANSAS/JEOPARDY]

KENNY, PHIL, TED. (*continued*) (*to the tune of "I'M BRING-ING HOME A BABY BUMBLE BEE."*)
BA YOPA DOPA DOPO YOPO YO YOPO DOPO YOPA
    DOPA DOPE
(*MUSIC out.*)

TED. What a time! And what a crowd! Yeah, we're cookin'
here tonight at The Funny Farm (*PHIL & KENNY: insane
laughter.*) because we're all COMMITTED (*PHIL & KENNY
do asylum inmates.*) to comedy. That's right. We're crazy.
You're crazy. And so are we. And why is that? Well—(*KENNY
whispers to PHIL. PHIL whispers to TED. TED whispers to the
audience. TED looks at PHIL. PHIL looks at KENNY. KENNY
starts after someone in the audience. TED and PHIL stop him.
PHIL feeds KENNY something that calms him down.*) I've just
been informed that the head talent scout from the Johnny Car-
son show is in our audience tonight, my good old buddy, Paris.
    PHIL.
FRANCE?
    TED.
NO, RICK (*hits PHIL*) PARIS
    KENNY.
HE'S IN FRANCE?
    TED.
THAT'S TWO FOR YOU. NOW THE REASON HE'S COME
TO THE FUNNY FARM IS THAT RICK (*hits PHIL again*)
PARIS IS LOOKING FOR
    TED, PHIL & KENNY.
A MARX BROTHERS RITZ BROTHERS THREE STOOGE
TYPE GANG OF FUNNY GUYS.
    TED. And in just a few moments, I know he's gonna be beside
himself with laughter. How will he get beside himself with
laughter?

(*All three look confused. We hear "Final Jeopardy" music. They
    silently discuss with animated gestures. KENNY makes
    buzzer sound.*)

TED, PHIL & KENNY. (*in unison*) We don't know.

TED. But that happens a lot here at The Funny Farm (*PHIL and KENNY: insane laughter.*) thanks to the many great stand-up comics who've played here ever since The Funny Farm (*insane laughter*) opened almost 6,000 years ago. And that is why we must pay homage (*pronounced "hoemahj"*)
PHIL & KENNY. WWWHAT?!
TED. And I do mean homage (*correct pronunciation*) to these great great heroes with this little bitty ditty..

(*TED, PHIL, and KENNY put on mock Gilbert and Sullivan costumes: TED is an admiral, PHIL, a pirate, and KENNY, a samurai.*)

[MUSIC #9: HISTORY OF STAND-UP COMEDY]

(*sings*)
SO MANY MANY MANY MANY YEARS AGO
BEFORE THE CREATION OF FIRE AND SNOW
THE UNIVERSE EXPLODED WITH THE FIRST
    APPLAUSE . . .
AND GOD MADE ALL THERE IS AND EVER WAS
    PHIL & KENNY.
GOD MADE EVERYTHING THERE EVER IS AND EVER
    WAS

    TED.
IN LESS THAN A WEEK HE MADE FISH AND FOLKS
    TED, PHIL & KENNY.
AND FROM THEN ON HE DECIDED TO REST
    TED.
AND HEAR A COUPLE OF JOKES
    KENNY.
SO HE SET THE SCENE
    PHIL.
FOR THE HEROES OF STAND-UP COMEDY
    TED, PHIL & KENNY.
TO DO THEIR BEST ROUTINES

    PHIL.
FIRST ADAM LAUGHED AND HELD HIS RIB
    TED.
WHILE EVE MADE CRACKS ON WOMEN'S LIB
    KENNY.
THEN NOAH BUILT A FLOATING ZOO

TED, PHIL & KENNY.
AND ABRAHAM BECAME A JEW
MOSES HAD FUN WITH A TALKING BURNING BUSH
DAVID SENT GOLIATH CRASHING ON HIS TUSH

ON HIS TUSH
BURNING BUSH
FLOATING ZOO
BECAME A JEW
WOMEN'S LIB
HELD HIS RIB
OH OH OH

   TED.
WHEN SOCRATES SAID "KNOW THYSELF" PEOPLE
   HAD TO PEE
   PHIL.
WHEN BUDDA SAT AND GOT REAL FAT IT KILLED
   THE JAPANESE
   KENNY.
WHEN JESUS SAW THE WORLD TO COME PEOPLE
   NEARLY DIED
   TED & PHIL.
CAESAR GAVE A SENATE SPEECH THAT NEARLY
RIPPED HIS SIDE

RIPPED HIS SIDE
NEARLY DIED
JAPANESE
HAD TO PEE
ON HIS TUSH
BURNING BUSH
FLOATING ZOO
BECAME A JEW
WOMEN'S LIB
HELD HIS RIB
OH OH OH (*KENNY leaves*) Uh oh.

(*TED and PHIL try to remember what's next.*)

   TED.
COLUMBUS PLAYED THE QUEEN WITH STYLE
   PHIL. (*Flubbing it—it's KENNY's line*)
HOO HA HOO HA

TED.
"MIKE" ANGELO DREW NUDES ON WALLS
TED & PHIL.
AND GALILEO DROPPED HIS BALLS
(*They watch imaginary balls bounce to the sound of a woodblock.*)
PHIL.
MACHIAVELLI MADE THE PRINCE THE LAUGHING
    STOCK . . .
(THE EIGHTH KING HENRY TOLD THE CHURCH TO
TAKE A WALK . . .)

(*MUSIC falls apart as TED sees RICK PARIS leave. He runs off after him through the audience.*)

TED. Rick! Paris! Just a second, Paris. It's just a joke, man. He'll be back. Come on, Paris. Give us a break, man. (*TED exits. The Band starts up again.*)
PHIL.
GEORGE WASHINGTON MADE PEOPLE SNORT BY
POWDERING HIS NOSE—
Whoa! Whoa! Wait a minute—hold it! (*He cuts off the Band.*) What the hell am I doing up here? Look, this wasn't my idea, you know. You see, Ted thought this guy Paris was really gonna go crazy for—but then Kenny, Kenny went and—look, I hate Gilbert and Sullivan! And I hope you had a good time. Goodnight.

(*PHIL walks off. KENNY enters, white neutral mask on top of his head. He has his tape recorder, presses the play/record button.*)

TED. (*from audience*) Hey guys, Phil . . . Kunin . . . Kenny?

(*KENNY disappears, TED comes on stage.*)

TED. Kenny, I know you're here. Are you all right? Come on Kenny, I got to talk to you. All right? I'm going to find Kunin. Meet us at Columbus Circle in an hour, O.K.? And Kenny, this is important.

(*TED exits. KENNY reappears and pushes the "play" button on his tape recorder.*)

KENNY'S VOICE. (*tape*) Shay! Kidsh! Ya wanna have a great time?! Yeah, yeah, I wanna have a great time. C'mere. Pull down your pants and bend over! (*sound of whip cracking*)

KENNY. That's sick. (*sets up mock confessional and plays both roles:*)

Bless me, Father, for I have sinned.

(*Offstage laughter—KENNY as a priest mimes laughing.*) Go on my son.

Father, I deserted my friends.

(*Laughter*) Yes my son.

And Father, I tried to kill someone.

(*Laughter*) Who was that, my son?

Myself, Father.

(*Laughter*) Well what's wrong with that because *you're killing me!!* (*Hysterical laughter*)

[MUSIC #10: DREAMS OF HEAVEN]

(*A tape recording of hysterical laughter joins KENNY. KENNY stops laughing. The taped laughter continues, getting louder and louder and reverberating. KENNY turns off the tape recorder but the laughter continues. PROJECTION of Funny Farm fades out. PROJECTION of nebulae star clusters comes up. He covers his ears and the laughter fades away. He sings:*)

KENNY.
CLATTER ALL AROUND YOU
SILENCE IN BETWEEN
VISIONS OF A WELL KNOWN PLACE
NO ONE ELSE HAS SEEN
THE CROWD IS GETTING RESTLESS
TO HEAR WHAT YOU WILL SAY
THE LIGHT IS REACHING TOWARD YOU
BUT YOU'RE NOT PREPARED TO STAY

THUNDERSTORM SURROUNDS YOU
EMPTY AT THE CORE
THE DANGER OF AN UNKNOWN PLACE
YOU HAD KNOWN BEFORE
THE CROWD IS GETTING ANGRY
THEY KNOW YOU'VE GONE AWAY
THE LIGHT IS COMING TOWARD YOU

BUT YOU TURN THE OTHER WAY

I TRY EACH NIGHT TO GET HERE
BUT MY BODY WON'T LET GO
THERE IS A PLACE FOR ME THEY SAID
BUT THE CALL COMES FROM BELOW
IT'S KILLING ME TO LIVE EACH DAY
WHEN I KNOW I HAVE TO DIE
BUT I'LL TRY . . .
DREAMS OF HEAVEN WILL HELP ME GET BY

SOMEWHERE A HIDDEN SUN
IN ME IT HAS BEGUN
HIS WILL WILL BE DONE

LAUGHTER ALL AROUND YOU
MIRTHLESS IN ITS WAKE
THE TERROR OF A NEW FOUND PLACE
YOU WILL NOT FORSAKE
THE CROWD IS GOING CRAZY
AT THE MENTION OF YOUR NAME
THE LIGHT IS PASSING THROUGH YOU
YOU WILL NEVER BE THE SAME

IT TOOK EACH NIGHT TO GET HERE
NOW MY SOUL IS ALL ABLAZE
AND EVERY PLACE CRIES OUT TO ME
WITH LOVE AND TEARFUL PRAISE
IT'S AGONY TO HAVE TO KISS
THIS LIFE GOODBYE
BUT I'LL TRY
DREAMS OF HEAVEN WILL HELP ME GET BY
DREAMS OF HEAVEN WILL HELP ME GET BY

(*BLACKOUT.*)

(*Lights up. The Comedy Club set is gone. Above,* PROJECTIONS
of night in Central Park. KENNY *is playing with a zombie
ball [a.k.a. magician's floating ball].* PHIL *runs on, fit to be
tied.*)

PHIL. (*to KENNY*) What the hell is the matter with you, man, huh? I mean, you made us look like a couple of — (*KENNY with zombie ball darts away from PHIL.*) — you love to do that, don't you? Look, I just want to talk to you for a — will you hold still for one second — I mean you really messed us up back there — Will you cut that out! I'm just trying to — I can't even get one — AAAUGH!

(*KENNY zombie balls away. TED comes in with ghetto blaster going full blast.*)

[MUSIC #10A: RAP #3]

TED.
NOW YOU MAY BE UPSET
AND SEEIN' RED
BUT TRY TO CALM DOWN
AND LISTEN UP TO TED
NOW TONIGHT
WE WERE ON THE LINE
BUT WE STARTED COOL
AND WE STARTED FINE
THEN KENNY WENT OFF,
WE WERE IN A SPOT
AND WHEN PARIS LEFT,
WE DIDN'T KNOW WHAT HE THOUGHT
BUT GUESS WHAT PARIS THOUGHT?
    PHIL.
HE HATED US.
    TED.
HELL NO, HE WANTS TO GIVE US A SHOT.
    PHIL.
WHAT?
    TED.
HE WANTS TO GIVE US—
    PHIL.
A SHOT?
    TED.
YEAH.
    PHIL.
ON CARSON?
    TED.
YEAH.

PHIL.
WAIT. WE'RE GONNA BE ON CARSON?

TED.
PARIS GAVE HIS WORD AND PARIS NEVER LIES
WE'RE A MARX BROTHERS RITZ BROTHERS

TED & PHIL.
THREE STOOGE TYPE GANG OF FUNNY GUYS

PHIL.
HOLY SHIT, WE DID IT, MAN!

TED.
WE DID IT, MAN!

TED AND PHIL.
WE DID IT!
YEAH!

PHIL.
YEAH, ALL RIGHT, YOU AND ME!

TED.
YOU, ME AND KENNY.

PHIL. Whoa! Wait a minute. (*shuts off ghetto blaster*) Whaddya mean, you, me and Kenny? The guy ran out on us.

TED. Yeah, he sure did, and Paris thought it was funny as Hell.

PHIL. Wait a minute! Wait a minute!

TED. The looks on our faces. Paris thought it was a great bit.

PHIL. Hold it man, just hold it a second—

TED. He's nuts about Brewster.

PHIL. What are you talking about?

TED. "The three of us," he said, "the perfect combination. Pure chemistry."

PHIL. Look man, there's no way this guy is gonna—

TED. It's the three of us or nothing.

PHIL. According to you or Paris?

TED. Both.

PHIL. This is great! Boy, do I need this! I mean I quit law school to become a stand-up comic. Right? And my girlfriend really wants to have this baby. And now that we've got the biggest break we could ask for—(*KENNY does a birdcall. PHIL reacts*)—a one-in-a-million shot on national T.V.—(*KENNY does another birdcall. PHIL reacts.*)—I've got to count on this guy over here. (*KENNY does yet another birdcall. PHIL is beside himself.*) A guy who's probably gonna do tropical bird calls . . . in the middle of our routine . . . and then fly out into the audience! And that's only if he shows up!

TED. (*Turns ghetto blaster back on; MUSIC now from onstage speaker.*)
HEY, KEEP IT COOL
AND KEEP IT LIGHT
HE'LL BE O.K.
IF WE HANDLE THIS RIGHT
BECAUSE IT ALL DEPENDS ON BREWSTER!
NOW KENNY
WE GOTTA STICK TOGETHER
WE MAKE A TEAM
CUZ WE WERE COOKIN' TOGETHER
AND IT'S GONNA GET BETTER
NOW WE'VE GOT AN OPPORTUNITY
TO RISE FROM OBSCURITY
I'm asking you as a friend.
KENNY.
O.K.
TED. (*not hearing*)
I want you to think this through
KENNY.
O.K.
PHIL. (*not hearing either*)
You gotta help us out.
KENNY.
O.K.
TED. (*still not hearing*)
BUT ONLY IF YOU HAVE NO DOUBT
KENNY.
I SAID O.K.!
TED.
WHAT?
KENNY.
ALL RIGHT!
TED.
Whoa! Wait a minute! (*turns off the ghetto blaster*) The three of us? Together? On Carson?

(*KENNY turns ghetto blaster back on with his foot and starts bopping to the beat.*)

KENNY.
YEAH
IT'S O.K.
IT'S ALL RIGHT
YOU WANNA BE A TEAM
YOU WANNA LIVE A DREAM
YOU WANNA TOUCH OF FAME
YOU WANNA STAKE A CLAIM
WELL IT'S ALL RIGHT, IT'S O.K., CUZ IN THE END,
YOU'RE BOUND TO FIND IT'S REALLY ALL THE SAME

(*KENNY does bizarre dance movements. TED gets off on
    KENNY. PHIL doesn't know what to make of him, but
    eventually joins in.*)

IT'S ALL THE SAME TO ME.
IF YOU WANNA STAY HERE
OR PLAY SOMETHING OVER THERE,
WELL I DON'T CARE.
IF YOU WANNA LIVE A DREAM . . .
THEN WE'RE A TEAM
    TED.
WE'RE A TEAM?
    KENNY.
WE'RE A TEAM!
    PHIL.
WE'RE A TEAM!
    TED & KENNY.
WE'RE A TEAM!
    PHIL.
WE'RE A TEAM!
    TED, PHIL & KENNY.
WE'RE A COMEDY TEAM!
AND . . .
IF WE PULL OUR SHIT TOGETHER
AND WE WATCH OUR FUCKING LANGUAGE
AND WE MAKE OUR CRAP ACCESSIBLE
THE NEXT THING YOU KNOW
WE'LL BE SUPERSTARS!
    KENNY.
SUPERSTARS?
    PHIL.
SUPER

TED.
SUPERSTAR
  KENNY.
STAR?
  TED & PHIL.
YEAH!
  KENNY.
I DON'T WANNA BE A SUPER—
  TED & PHIL.
YOU DON'T WANNA BE A SUPER—
  KENNY.
I DON'T WANNA—
  TED.
YOU DON'T WANNA—
  PHIL.
HE DON'T WANNA—
  TED, PHIL & KENNY.
WE DON'T WANNA—
NO! NO!
NO! NO! NO! NO!

[MUSIC #11: SUPERSTAR III]

(PROJECTIONS *of airport scenes.*)

(*Sing*)
I SAY NOW
I DON'T WANNA BE A SUPERSTAR
  KENNY.
LATEST GREATEST PHENOMENA YEAH
  TED, PHIL & KENNY.
DON'T WANNA
SYMBOLIZE AMERICA
  TED.
I'D RATHER SPEND MY LIFE AN UNKNOWN STAND-UP

(*Dance break*)

  TED, PHIL & KENNY.
DON'T WANNA RUN
DON'T WANNA RUN NO JET SET PACE
DON'T WANNA SEE, DON'T WANNA

SEE MY PICTURE EVERY PLACE
  PHIL.
DIE ALONE AND IN DISGRACE
  TED, PHIL & KENNY.
OH NO
I DON'T WANNA BE DON'T WANNA BE A SUPERSTAR
I DON'T WANNA BE DON'T WANNA BE A SUPERSTAR
I DON'T WANNA BE DON'T WANNA BE A SUPERSTAR

(*BLACKOUT*)

(PROJECTIONS *of "Flight 737 boarding," "Fasten Seat Belts" and "No Smoking" flash on and off.*)

VOICEOVER. This is the final boarding call for Flight 737 to Los Angeles. The plane is ready for take-off. Will a Mr. Steve, Mr. Spike, and Mr. Dirtball please report to Gate 14.

[MUSIC #11A: TWILIGHT PLANES]

(*Lights up, revealing PHIL and KENNY in the interior of a plane. TED comes on. TED plays head steward while PHIL and KENNY play demonstrating stewardesses complete wtih emergency exit maps and oxygen masks. They are all a little high.*)

TED. Hi there. How ya doin'? My name is "Ted," and I'll be your host today on Flight 737 to Los Angeles. Please observe our cabin attendants, Philly and Kenny, as they self-consciously pantomime our safety features. Should you need oxygen, an oxygen mask will drop into your lap. Put it on, relax, and breath normally; you'll have a full ten seconds worth of air so you can tidy up loose ends before you kiss your ass goodbye. Our seat belts fit right across your laps with buckles that open and close. Like this. We'd like to ask the gentlemen not to stand up without releasing your buckle or you'll squash your balls. The exit doors are designated on the blueprints in your seat pockets. Please don't open these doors while the plane is in flight, or we'll all be sucked out of the cabin, flail around helplessly in the air, smash into the ground, and die. We hope you enjoy your flight and should we make it to Los Angeles, we'll be happy to help you locate the city where we've sent your luggage. (*TED, PHIL and*

KENNY *dip as the plane seems to have taken a dive.*) It's all right, ladies and gentlemen. You can relax. We're in good hands. The captain of this plane happens to be the last surviving kamikaze pilot of World War II. Ooh, for a second there it was just like "The Twilight Zone," wasn't it? (*"Twilight Zone" music*)

PHIL. (*Rod Serling*) Consider, if you will, this extraordinary juxtaposition of avocations. The Japanese suicide pilot . . .

KENNY. (*Japanese horror film victim*) Aw shit! We in big tlouble!

PHIL. And the American stand-up comic.

TED. Let's all have sex.

PHIL. Through some bizarre twist of fate, we find ourselves faced with stand-up pilots who tell bad jokes . . .

KENNY. Ret's arr have sex.

PHIL. And Kamikaze comics willing to sacrifice themselves for eternal glory.

(*Before TED can speak, TED, PHIL and KENNY jerk to the side as the plane swerves.*)

[MUSIC #12: KAMIKAZE KABARET]

PHIL. Look guys, I don't wanna do a Gilbert and Sullivan patter song on Carson. I wanna be a Kamikaze Comic.

TED. You wanna crash on Carson?

PHIL. I wanna explode on Carson. Look, guys whatever we do, that's what people are gonna know us for.

TED. You're right, we gotta do something outrageous.

PHIL. Something hangin' on the edge.

KENNY. Over the edge.

TED, PHIL. Yeah.

PHIL. Let's do it.

TED. Why not? This is America, isn't it? (*Gong sounds. They look at each other.*) Let's go for broke. (*sings*)
FLASHING ON THE SCREEN
ON A LATE NIGHT T.V. SPOT
IF WE'RE GONNA GO, WE'RE GOING ALL THE WAY
THE ODDS ARE SET AGAINST US
BUT WE GOTTA TAKE OUR SHOT
DOIN' KAMIKAZE KABARET

PHIL.
SHAKIN' IN OUR SHOES
YOU KNOW WE GOT A LOT TO LOSE
THEY MAY CUT US OFF AND ASK US NOT TO STAY
BUT SINCE WE GET TO CHOOSE
YOU KNOW WE'D RATHER PAY OUR DUES
DOIN' KAMIKAZE KABARET
TED & PHIL.
WE'RE GONNA GO GO GO FOR BROKE
NOTHING'S GONNA STAND IN OUR WAY
TED, PHIL & KENNY.
WE'RE GONNA GO GO GO FOR BROKE
DOIN' KAMIKAZE KABARET
KENNY.
STICKIN' TO OUR GUNS
WE GOTTA BE PREPARED TO RUN
IF WE HIT THE GROUND
WE'LL BURST RIGHT INTO FLAME
AS THREE FUSE INTO ONE,
WE CAN SAY WE HAD SOME FUN
DOIN' KAMIKAZE KABARET
TED, PHIL & KENNY.
WE'RE GONNA GO GO GO FOR BROKE
NOTHING'S GONNA STAND IN OUR WAY
WE'RE GONNA GO GO GO FOR BROKE
DOIN' KAMIKAZE KABARET

(*TED, PHIL, and KENNY step off plane interior, and it disappears behind them.*)

STRIKING FROM THE DARK
WE GOTTA SPEAK STRAIGHT FROM THE HEART
PHIL.
EXPOSING WHAT WE DO AND SAY
KENNY.
WE GOTTA TAKE THE CHANCE
TED.
THAT WE MAY BLOW OURSELVES
TED, PHIL & KENNY.
AWAY—HAY—HAY

FLASHIN' ON THE SCREEN
SHAKIN' IN OUR SHOES
STICKIN' TO OUR GUNS
YEAH!

FLASHIN' ON THE—
SHAKIN' IN OUR—
STICKIN' TO OUR GUNS
YEAH!

FLASHIN'
SHAKIN'
STICKIN'
WHOA! YEAH! YEAH! YEAH! YEAH! YEAH!

WE'RE GONNA GO GO GO FOR BROKE
NOTHING'S GONNA STAND IN OUR WAY
WE'RE GONNA GO GO GO FOR BROKE
DOIN' KAMIKAZE KABARET YEAH YEAH!

WE'RE GONNA GO GO GO GO GO FOR BROKE
NOTHING'S GONNA STAND IN OUR WAY
WE'RE GONNA GO GO GO FOR BROKE
DOIN' KAMIKAZE KABARET HEY! HEY!
WE'RE GONNA GO GO GO FOR BROKE!!

(PROJECTIONS *of TED, PHIL and KENNY freefalling without
parachutes.*)

(*BLACKOUT*)

END ACT ONE

ACT TWO

[MUSIC #13: ACT II OPENING]

In the darkness, we hear a blaring, jazzy "Tonight Show" band musical interlude. Lights on the band. Big finish. Drumroll.

TED. (*off-stage on mike*) Let us return to the 1950's.

(PROJECTION: *three photos of Ike in official poses: at Inauguration, etc.*)

The world was readying itself to be able to be poised on the brink of nuclear annihilation.

(PROJECTION, C., *of "war board" map of the world, as in Act I, but with only a handful of nuclear warheads; on L., Krushchev slamming his shoe; on R., Ike golfing*)

Millions of people had jobs, homes, and a future.

(PROJECTIONS: *rows and rows of factory workers doing the same job; rows and rows of identical tract houses; and an audience watching a 3-D movie*)

The situation looked hopeful.

(PROJECTION, L., *of John F. Kennedy in the 50's as Congressman; R., Elvis; and finally, C., Marilyn Monroe*)

And very serious.

(PROJECTION *montage: Howdy Doody, Bozo the Clown, Ike golfing, Captain Kangaroo, Pinky Lee, Ike golfing, Milton Berle, Jerry Lewis, Joe McCarthy, children practicing bomb drills at school, Ike golfing, Brando, James Dean, Ike golfing, other 50's images interspersed with Ike golfing*)

Until three guys!

(PROJECTIONS: *head shots of all three with "Who, us?" expressions*)

Three very silly guys!

(PROJECTIONS *of baby pictures of TED, L., PHIL, C. and KENNY, R., Each with ballooned dialogue "Who, me?" superimposed.*)

Came into the world and spent the next thirty years preparing for this very moment. Ladies and gentlemen, the Tonight Show is happy to bring you Ted Klausterman, Phil Kunin, and Kenny Brewster!

[MUSIC #14: AMERICAN DREAM]

(*Lights come up on TED at piano. TED as Baptist preacher, Jerry Lee Lewis 1950's hard rocker, sings:*)

BROTHERS AND SISTERS
SONS AND DAUGHTERS
LISTEN TO ME CHILDREN
LISTEN TO ME

(*KENNY and PHIL enter as back-up singer/dancers.* PROJECTIONS *of TED, PHIL and KENNY as little boys.*)

THERE'S SOMETHIN' DEEP WITHIN YOU
THAT'S CRYIN' IN PAIN
IT CALLS YOU LATE AT NIGHT
BY YOUR FIRST NAME
AND IF YOU SAW IT YOU WOULD HOLLER AND
  SCREAM
CUZ IT'S THE VERY SCARY HAIRY AHAHMERICAN
  DREAM

YOU USED TO SING ABOUT THE NAVY
TELL IT TO THE MARINES
EVERYBODY PASSED THE GRAVY
CUZ WE ALL HAD THE MEANS
TO RIDE LIKE KINGS AND QUEENS
  TED, PHIL & KENNY.
ON CHEAP GASOLINE

TED.
CUZ IT'S THE VERY SCARY HAIRY AHAHMERICAN
DREAM
(*spoken*) I'm talkin' about life in the 50's, brothers and sisters.
A time when greasy-haired men said they were "Boss," pony-
tailed women said they were virgins, and everybody was lying.
And we all had a dream: to make a lot of money selling
aluminum siding and have 2.3 kids called "Wally" and "The Bea-
ver." (*KENNY and PHIL exit. TED sings.*)
BUT THEN THE BEAT GENERATION
THE BEAT GENERATION
CRIED OUT WITH
COOL, HIP, SWINGING, JAZZ TALK
POETRY AND RAGE
THE 50's CAME OF AGE
AND PEOPLE WHO WERE SAGE
AGREED ABOUT-ONE-THING

(*PHIL enters as a 1960's folksinger-activist Bob Dylan type,
plays guitar and harmonica. TED puts on beads and headband and backs him up. KENNY enters, smoking an imaginary joint.*)

PHIL.
IT WAS A VERY SCARY HAIRY AHAHMERICAN DREAM

(PROJECTIONS *of TED, PHIL and KENNY in 60's garb in their
young teens.*)

NOW BROTHERS AND SISTERS
AND FRIENDS NEWLY MET
YOU MUST LISTEN TO THOSE WHO'VE NOT LEARNED
   TO HATE YET
OUR CHILDREN KNOW SOMETHING THAT MAKES
   THEIR EYES DANCE
THE WORLD CAN BE MAGIC IF YOU GIVE IT A CHANCE
IT'S A VISION MUCH SWEETER THAN CAKE AND ICE
   CREAM
IT'S THE LONG AGO PROMISED AMERICAN DREAM
(*spoken*) I'm talking about life in the 60's, people. A time when
if you grew long hair and a beard you were called "groovy," even
if you were a woman. And we all had a dream: to give away a lot

of money to just about everybody . . . and watch Link get pissed off on "The Mod Squad." (*MUSIC pause.*) And then the Flower Power, cult crazy Manson family snuffed it out with Helter Skelter blood stains. (*KENNY exits, disillusioned with the 60's. TED follows. PHIL sings.*)
SO INSANE
WE COULDN'T COMPREHEND
BUT WE KNEW
THE 60's HAD TO END
(*spoken*) It was time to change the scene.

(*KENNY enters in a 1970's white ice cream disco suit, sings Bee Gee style.*)

KENNY.
BUT NOT THE LONG AGO PROMISED AMERICAN DREAM

(PROJECTIONS *of TED, PHIL, and KENNY as slick, young adults of the '70's. TED and PHIL come back on, wearing white disco jackets, and join KENNY.*)

TED, PHIL & KENNY. (*à la The Bee Gees*)
BROTHERS AND SISTERS
MOTHERS AND FATHERS
LISTEN TO THE RHYTHM OF YOUR OWN DESIRES
SEE YOURSELF AS SOMEONE EVERYBODY ADMIRES
AH AH HAVE SOME FUN
AND LOOK OUT FOR NUMBER ONE
KENNY.
YOU CAN GET YOUR ACT TOGETHER
KENNY & TED.
YOU CAN SAY YOU NEED SPACE
TED, PHIL & KENNY.
YOU MUST ALWAYS WIN WHETHER OR NOT YOU'RE IN THE RACE
KENNY.
FOR AS LONG AS YOU SAVE FACE
TED & PHIL.
AH AH AH
KENNY.
YOU WILL REIGN

TED, PHIL & KENNY.
SUPREME
IN THE SURVIVAL OF THE FITTEST THE AMERICAN
    DREAM

KENNY. (*spoken*) I'm talking about life in the 70's: a time
when men intimidated women . . . and then used their hair-
dryers. And we all had a dream: to invest a lot of money in a
tropical island and have a French horny midget that says, "Boss,
Boss, de plane! de plane!"

TED, PHIL & KENNY. (*sing*)
BUT THEN THE NEW RIGHT BIBLE THUMPING
SPIRIT SQUASHERS
TRIED TO TAKE CONTROL
WITH SMILES AND PETTY PHRASES
ECONOMIC MAZES
THE DIE WAS CAST
THE 70's WERE PAST
(PROJECTION *of huge flag*)
WHAT DID THIS MEAN
TO THE NEVER ENDING SEARCH
FOR THE AMERICAN DREAM
(*They rip off their velcroed pullaway pants.*)
    TED, KENNY.
WE NEED A NEW GENERATION OF
    PHIL.
A NEW GENERATION OF
    TED, PHIL & KENNY.
HEROES
AND WE NEED A NEW
WE NEED A NEW AMERICAN DREAM
(*They rip off their shirts, leaving them in boxer shorts and tennis
shoes.*)
IT'S SOMETHING DEEP WITHIN YOU THAT'S CRYING
    WITH PAIN
GOTTA REACH OUT TO YOUR BROTHERS
FREE THAT INNER SPIRIT
SAY THAT WE CAN MAKE THINGS CHANGE
WHEN WE LEARN TO DREAM
THE VERY SCARY HAIRY
DREAM THE SAME
SURVIVAL OF THE FITTEST
LEARN TO DREAM THE SAME
LONG AGO PROMISED

(PROJECTIONS *of 3 guys simulating Iwo Jima flag-raising* (R.), *their faces superimposed on Mt. Rushmore leaving Lincoln* (L.) *and in* C. *all 3 wearing a giant "Who Me?" shirt with their boxer shorts around their ankles.*)
AMERICAN DREAM!

(*TED soaks in the applause. PHIL is pleasantly surprised by it. And KENNY withdraws inside himself. Lights change. Dressing room set appears. TED and PHIL both hug KENNY, then start getting dressed.*)

[MUSIC #15: BREATHLESS & CONFUSED]

TED. You guys were great.

(PROJECTIONS *of crowds.*)

PHIL. I can't believe we did it. We really did it.
KENNY. I can't believe it.
TED. Did you see the look on Johnny's face? He thought he was gonna see—
TED & PHIL. —a Gilbert and Sullivan patter song!
PHIL. I can't believe they let us get away with it.
KENNY. I can't believe it.
TED. Ed was laughing and waving to us.
KENNY. Who's Ed?
PHIL. Y'know that buddy of yours from Yale? Ol' Ricky Paris. He was standing there on the side going, "What're they doing?! What are they doing?! I thought the guy was gonna pop a gut!
TED. Yeah, that's Paris, man.
KENNY. Yeah, that's Paris, man.
TED. (*puts his hand on KENNY's shoulders*) Thanks Kenny. (*pause*) Ed MacMahon.
KENNY. Who?
TED. You hear that guys. They're pounding on the dressing room door. (PROJECTIONS *of more crowds*) They're calling our names. They want us to come out.
PHIL. (*sees crazy, adoring throng; sings:*)
BREATHLESS AND CONFUSED
FINGERS POINT TO YOU.
TED.
NO MORE FEAR

PHIL.
NO MORE FEAR
TED.
THE WORLD IS HERE
TO LOOK AT YOU
KENNY.
OUR VOICES GETTING LOUDER NOW
CHILLS UP AND DOWN OUR SPINE
PHIL.
I FEEL THE JOY OF LIVING
FROM THEIR DANCING EYES TO MINE
TED.
OUR HEARTS ARE FILLED WITH DREAMS
OF PRIZES TO BE WON
TED, PHIL & KENNY.
THE TIME FOR BETTER TIMES HAS JUST BEGUN

(PROJECTIONS: *Blurred abstracts of roller coaster, blinking on and off, constantly moving and changing.*)

(*TED, PHIL, and KENNY put on sunglasses.*)

TED, PHIL & KENNY.
CHAINS AND LEVERS PULL YOU
STRUGGLING UP THE HILL YOU
KNOW THE DROP COULD KILL YOU
HANG ON TIGHT UNTIL
YOU WANT IT TO END
WHAT A RIDE
PHIL, KENNY.
WHAT A RIDE
KENNY.
WHAT A—

(*The KOMEDY CLUB WEST set has now rolled on. It is the L.A. counterpart to the KOMEDY KLUB EAST, and is depicted by* PROJECTIONS *of Los Angeles, THE KOMEDY KLUB WEST logo, and three stools on a bare stage.*)

TED. (*does ominous-sounding, terror picture, live voiceover while PHIL and KENNY do House of Horrors acting*) And now! Just when you thought it was safe to be a hit on The Johnny Carson Show, The Komedy Klub West is proud to present Ted Klausterman, Phil Kunin and Kenny Brewster in KILLER AGENTS! (*Horror movie thunderstorm is heard.*)

PHIL. Guys, I think we're gonna need a good agent . . .

(*During the following, TED, PHIL and KENNY put on different hats, glasses, and scarves, and do character voices.*)

TED. (*tough voice*) Boys, we just saw you on Carson last night and you were terrific. Here's my card; Harry Gardner. And this is my partner, Elliot Ross. Tell 'em Elliot.

PHIL. (*Jewish accent*) I'm his partner, Elliot Ross; listen: you boys are pretty good. But you're gonna need somebody watching out for your best interests.

KENNY. Yeah, but — but — but —

TED. (*Gardner*) Because we think you boys are gonna be big stars. Tell 'em Elliot.

PHIL. (*Ross*) Because we think you boys are gonna be big stars.

TED. (*as himself*) Well, I guess we need somebody who really knows the ropes.

KENNY. (*Grandad*) Don't waste your time frying small potatoes, I'm Bobby Bud and this is my assistant, Lance Wizell; Lance, straighten these young fellows out, O.K.?

TED. (*just starting out*) O.K., I'm very happy to meet you, O.K. We're with the William Morris Agency, O.K., and as you know, we're the largest in the world and we feel you gentlemen need a lot of clout behind you to get your careers off to the right start —

PHIL. I don't know what to say.

KENNY. (*Richard Simmons Swish. — T. Robert Fish*) Of course you don't know what to say. That's why we do all the talking for you. I'm T. Robert Fish and this is my associate, Freddy Footlick. Fill 'em in, Toots.

PHIL. (*pipe; fruity yuppie*) You three are marvelous! And if we can work together, I think it'll be fabou!

TED. (*Harry Gardner*) Fabou shmabou. You need agents with experience. Tell 'em Elliot!

PHIL. (*Elliot Ross*) Fabou shmabou. Experience!

KENNY. (*Bobby Bud*) Experience. I've got more experience than everybody's grandmother! Lance!

TED. (*Lance Wizell*) That's clout! You need clout!

PHIL. Yeah, we need clout.

KENNY. (*T. Robert Fish*) We've got plenty of clout. Fill 'em in Footlick!

PHIL. (*Freddy Footlick*) I think it'll be fabou!

TED. (*Harry Gardner*) Listen boys, work with us, we'll get you a T.V. series right away. Tell 'em Elliot.

PHIL. (*Elliot Ross*) A T.V. series right away.

TED, PHIL & KENNY. Yeah, but, but, but—(*Harry Gardner, Elliot Ross, Bobby Bud*)

BOYS A MARX BROTHERS RITZ BROTHERS THREE STOOGE TYPE GANG OF FUNNY GUYS T.V. SERIES!

TED. This is a tough choice.

KENNY. Yeah.

PHIL. We need time to think about it.

[MUSIC #15½: JEOPARDY MUSIC]

TED, PHIL & KENNY.(*Lance, Ross, Fish*) Time's up!

KENNY. (*Fish*) Sign with us.

TED. (*Gardner*) Sign with us.

PHIL, KENNY. (*Footlick, Bud*) Sign with . . . (*They both have heart attacks.*)

TED. (*Gardner*) Welcome aboard boys. Listen, we just got you a T.V. series. It's called "Hello, Fellas." Undercover cops. Great stuff. It'll be a big hit and you'll be making a lotta money for the next seven years. Tell 'em, Elliot.

PHIL. (*Ross*) . . . Seven years. Here's the contract. Sign it and take it to the studio. You're gonna be taping the title song and rehearsing the first episode in half an hour. See ya there.

(*The Club set rolls back through the ribbon curtain and disappears.*)

[MUSIC #15A: TAPING TITLE SONG]

(PROJECTIONS *of streets. During the following, TED holds a contract that gets grabbed and snatched by all three.*)

TED. (*rhythmic patter*)
TAPING TITLE SONG AND—

KENNY.

REHEARSING FIRST EPISODE

TED.

HEY, WE GOT A SERIES!

KENNY.

YEAH, WE GOT A T.V. SERIES

PHIL.

HALF AN HOUR

SEVEN YEARS

WAIT A MINUTE

JUST A SECOND!

Now what's going on?

TED.

WELL, WE GOT A T.V. SERIES

KENNY.

YEAH, WE GOT A T.V. SERIES

PHIL.

YEAH, I KNOW WE GOT A T.V. SERIES

SEVEN YEARS WE GOT A SERIES

Don't sign that yet!

TED. Look, relax guy, the contract's fine. It's the best we're gonna get.

PHIL. Let me read it.

TED. O.K. So read it. I thought you didn't want to be a lawyer.

PHIL. I don't want to get screwed.

KENNY. He don't want to get screwed.

PHIL. And I don't wanna be tied up for seven years in a piece of crap.

TED.

WHAT PIECE OF CRAP? HAVE YOU READ THE SCRIPT?

PHIL.

WELL, NO

TED.

ALL RIGHT

PHIL.

HAVE YOU READ THE SCRIPT?

TED.

WELL, NO

KENNY.

ALL RIGHT

TED & PHIL. (*to KENNY*)
HAVE YOU READ THE SCRIPT?
KENNY.
WHAT SCRIPT?
PHIL.
ALL RIGHT, NOW THAT'S MY POINT
TED.
WHAT POINT? LOOK
HERE'S OUR TICKET, IT'S IN OUR HANDS
IF WE MAKE THIS SERIES HOT
IT FITS RIGHT INTO OUR PLANS
KENNY.
GOOD POINT.
PHIL.
WHAT POINT? IF WE SIGN THIS THING,
THEY'LL OWN US, MAN
THAT'S 'MAKING IT' WRONG,
THAT'S TAKIN' THE WRONG KIND A
CHANCE
KENNY.
GOOD POINT
TED.
WHAT POINT? LOOK:
WE'LL DO IT FOR A YEAR,
MAKE A LOTTA DOUGH
FOLKS WILL KNOW WE'RE HERE
PHIL.
WE'LL HAVE NOWHERE ELSE TO GO
TED.
NOW YOU KNOW THAT WON'T BE SO
(*puts contract in pocket*)
CUZ: WE'RE GATHERING MOMENTUM
WE'LL RUSH ALONG
JUST THINK OF WHAT GOES RIGHT FOR US
IF NOTHING CAN GO WRONG
PHIL.
AND IF YOU'RE WRONG?
TED.
WHAT CAN GO WRONG?
TED, PHIL & KENNY.
WHAT CAN GO WRONG?

[MUSIC #16: PISTON POUNDING]

(*Roller coaster* PROJECTIONS. *They put on sunglasses and sing.*)

IT'S A WHITE KNUCKLE RACER
FEEL THE RUSH OF AIR
YOU WANNA BE A CLOUD CHASER
FINALLY YOU ARE THERE
POWER IN FLIGHT
CONQUERING SPEED
IT'S A HOT FLASH DELIGHT
IT'S EVERYTHING YOU NEED

QUICK ACCELERATION
ROCKET ESCALATION
PERILOUS DESTINATION
EXCITES THE NATION
WATCHING YOU FLY
WHAT A RIDE WHAT A RIDE
WHAT A—
WHAT A RIDE

(*Set wagon rolls out partially with scripts on it. They are now in the T.V. rehearsal studio. They pick the scripts up.* PROJECTION: *"REHEARSAL" flashes.*)

TED. (*to the powers that be, holding up contract*) Listen, we all signed the contract and we hear the script's really terrific, so, uh, we're excited to uh, get started. And I guess the best— Yeah. O.K. (*to KENNY*) You're first. (*KENNY does royal trumpet fanfare. TED laughs.*)

TED. (*to the powers that be*) Ha ha. That's Kenny. He uh— (*to KENNY*) Go ahead.

KENNY. I don't know about you, but I feel like Marvin Hamlisch in drag.

TED. (*laughs*) That's really terrif—(*He sees the powers that be aren't happy.*)

PHIL. I think my wig came from the third-runner up of the Bert Convy look-alike contest.

TED. Look, fellas, I know undercover detective work has its faults, but so does the San Andreas.

KENNY. (*shouting, off script*) IT'S NOT THE SAN AN-DREAS FAULT, IT'S MY FAULT. I SHOULD HAVE PLANTED MY LUNG LIKE SISTER PERPETUA TOLD ME TO. BLEAUGH! A cat throwing up: (*does a cat throwing up*)

TED. (*repeating*) Look, fellas, I know undercover detective work has its faults, but so does the San Andreas.

PHIL. (*reading script*) I don't care what the chief says, (*off script:*) the next time we bring in a rapist, I'm gonna pull out my butcher knife and chop off his chubby.

KENNY. Chubby?

PHIL. Chubby!

PHIL & KENNY. (*singing and dancing*) YEAH, LET'S TWIST AGAIN LIKE WE DID LAST SUMMER —

TED. (*to the powers that be*) We're just a little bit nervous, O.K.? We're just kinda loosening up. I guess if we just move on through it's probably — (*TED sees KENNY who's been mimicking him from behind.*)

PHIL. I don't care what the chief says, I refuse to go to second base in the line of duty.

KENNY. My girdle's killing me. (*drops to the ground as in cat attack*) EEEEEE! (*He flails around.*)

PHIL. "Praise the Lord and rise!" (*He hits KENNY.*)

TED. "Praise the Lord and rise!" (*He hits PHIL.*)

PHIL & TED. Cut to a commercial.

PHIL. He's dead, you killed him!

TED. He's dead. You killed him!

KENNY. (*little boy voice*) I'm dead, you killed me.

PHIL. (*Durante*) We gotta find a way to stop these killer girdles.

TED, PHIL & KENNY.
HA-CHA-CHA-CHA-CHA!

(*They look up and see the powers that be are upset.*)

TED. Guys, I think they want us to do the script the way it is. O.K.?

PHIL & KENNY. Sure! Sure!

PHIL. This is great. I've always dreamed of doing something like this for the next seven years. *This is great!*

TED. Take it easy.

PHIL. Whaddya mean, take it easy?! If you think — I mean,

first of all—but no—I listened to you—I mean, how the Hell am I supposed to take this piece of—There's no way we can—

TED. It's all right. He's still warming up.

PHIL. AAAUGH! (*to the powers that be*) I have to go to the bathroom.

KENNY. (*gets up*) Me too. (*PHIL and KENNY leave.*)

TED. (*to the powers that be*) They, uh, they had to go to the bathroom. That's why they were so uptight. Look, y'know we're used to doing our own material. Maybe we could talk a bit about the script. (*listens, then answers*) Well no, we've never done a series before, but—(*listens*) Yes, but—(*listens*) I understand, but—(*listens*) No, no, we can make this work. Just give us five minutes. O.K.? I promise you we'll come back and do it perfect. Thanks. (*He leaves.*)

(*BLACKOUT*)

VOICEOVER.
New on N.B.C., HELLO FELLAS!

[MUSIC #18: HELLO FELLAS]

(PROJECTIONS: *NBC logo, Hello Fellas logo*)

TED, PHIL & KENNY. (*sing*)
L.A. IS A SCARY PLACE
DETECTIVES OUGHTA KNOW
(PROJECTIONS: *(1) Shot of L.A.P.D. graphic or shield on building. (2) TED in police uniform. (3) PHIL in police uniform. (4) KENNY in police uniform.*)
THEY WORK AT SUCH A HARRIED PACE
THEY'RE ALWAYS ON THE GO
(PROJECTIONS: *(5) All three in police uniforms. (6) TED in drag, unsmiling. KENNY and PHIL still in uniform, laughing at him. (7) TED and PHIL in drag, unsmiling, KENNY in uniform, laughing at them. (8) TED, PHIL and KENNY in drag, all three unsmiling.*)
BUT HEY IN L.A.
WE CAN SAY
WE'RE GLAD TO MEET YA
(PROJECTIONS: *(9) All three working out in health club with nubile women. (10) TED, PHIL and KENNY punching out con-*

*struction workers who are ogling them. (11) TED ushering
PHIL and KENNY into the Ladies' Room. (12) TED, PHIL
and KENNY hitchhiking by showing their legs.)*

WE SURE COULD USE
THREE ZANY COPS LIKE YOU
(PROJECTIONS: *(13) TED, PHIL and KENNY drinking beer in a
bar. (14) All three arresting criminals at the bar. (15) All
three doing the Marilyn Monroe pose of dress blowing up
over an air grate. (16) KENNY on date with huge football
player. (17) PHIL smashing somebody against a wall. (18)
TED flirting with a lot of guys, who are lighting his cigarette, holding drinks, etc.)*

OOH OOH OOH
HELLO FELLAS
(PROJECTIONS: *(19) TED, PHIL and KENNY in police car, ad-
justing their wigs, make-up, etc. (20) They fix a flat tire on
the police car. (21) All three watching T.V. drinking beer in
their underwear. Their wigs and dresses and bras draped
over the T.V., couch and lamps. (22) All three fast asleep.
Superimposed T.V. credits over last several shots.)*

(We are now at the Comic Retreat. PROJECTIONS: *L.A. city
lights. Comic Retreat logo on center screen.)*

TED. (*voiceover*) *And now!* The Comic Retreat is proud to
present Ted Klausterman, Phil Kunin and Kenny Brewster in
Killer Careers On The Rise! (*Horror movie thunderstorm.
Lights up.*)

[MUSIC #19: MUZAK/DISCO II/CHORD]

*(The COMIC RETREAT set rolls out, with TED, PHIL, and
KENNY on it, sitting on stools. THE COMIC retreat is
another Los Angeles comedy spot, where they can do their
thing.)*

TED. (*Gardner*) Listen boys I'm proud of you, you're a big
hit. Tell 'em Elliot.
PHIL. (*Ross*) I'm proud of you boys, you're a bit hit.
TED. (*Gardner*) We're gonna put you boys on Carson again,
only this time in drag. Tell 'em Elliot.
PHIL. (*Ross*) In drag.

TED. (*Gardner*) The public's nuts about ya. The kids are crazy about ya. Tell 'em Elliot.

PHIL. (*Ross*) Crazy about ya. (*becomes PHIL again and signs autographs; disco music*)

KENNY. (*little boy*) Hey Mom, I'll have my dessert later. 'Hello, Fellas' is on.

TED. (*Gardner*) You're setting an example for the youth of America. Tell 'em Elliot.

PHIL. (*Ross*) An example for youth. (*becomes PHIL again, signs more autographs*)

KENNY. Hey Mom, when I grow up I wanna start wearing a dress, just like the guys on "Hello, Fellas." (*MUSIC out.*)

TED. (*Gardner*) Listen, boys, great news. You're gonna be doing a "Hello, Fellas" T.V. Special World Tour. Tell 'em Elliot.

PHIL. (*Ross*) A "Hello, Fellas" T.V. Special World Tour.

KENNY. (*Holds syringe. LENNY:*) Hey George, I don't wanna do a "Hello, Fellas" T.V. Special World Tour. (*GEORGE:*) You better do a "Hello, Fellas" T.V. Special World Tour or I'll turn you into a Giant Monkey. (*LENNY:*) O.K. George, I'll do it George! (*GEORGE:*) Too late! (*He injects himself. LENNY becomes a giant monkey.*)

TED. (*Gardner*) Listen boys, everybody's talking about the upcoming "Hello, Fellas" T.V. Special World Tour. It's gonna be terrific. Tell 'em Elliot.

PHIL. (*Ross*) Everybody's talking. It's gonna be terrific. I could kiss you meshugenahs. But I vant you should keep your noses clean. You know vat I mean. (*MUSIC up.*)

TED, PHIL & KENNY. (*sniff cocaine, sing*)
WHAT A RIDE

TED. (*Gardner*) What a great idea! A "Hello, Fellas" T.V. Special World Tour.

(*TED, KENNY, and the COMEDY CLUB disappear through the ribbon curtain.*)

PHIL. (*fast-talking AM disc jockey*) That's right! A "Hello Fellas" T.V. Special World Tour starring Ted Klausterman, Phil Kunin, and Kenny Brewster! This is Ridiculous Dick of W-H-A-T! WHAT! That's right! And I just want you to know that those wacky zany "Hello, Fellas" guys, Ted, Phil and Kenny, are close personal friends of you know who, Riddie Dickie! So if you want to meet these three madcap comics, then pop on over to the

Topanga Canyon shopping mall this weekend where Burger King will be hosting a Phil Kunin Look-Alike Contest. The winner gets a "Hello, Fellas" Home Video Game, batteries not included, and a very special weekend with the Kunins, Phil and Diane, at their home. Diane is six months pregnant and it looks like she's gonna have this baby this September September September, so, if you win the contest, they will name the child after you! And if they do, you'll also get: a set of "Hello, Fellas" miniature playdolls, a sturdy "Hello, Fellas" lunchbox, and two free tickets to the "Hello, Fellas" T.V. Special World Tour. WHAT?! That's right.

(*BLACKOUT*)

[MUSIC #20: THE WORLD TOUR]

(PROJECTION: *Hello Fellas T.V. Special World Tour*)

(*In the original production, the World Tour was done entirely with voice overs, projections, and live voices on backstage mikes. The World Tour can also be done with whatever live performances are deemed desirable.*)

TED. (*voiceover*) Ladies and gentlemen: The "Hello, Fellas" T.V. Special World Tour starring Ted Klausterman, Phil Kunin, and Kenny Brewster!

(*Big T.V. comedy special type musical verison of "Hello, Fellas" theme.* PROJECTIONS: *TED, PHIL and KENNY on the cover of T.V. Guide holding a globe. TED, PHIL and KENNY on the cover of TIME magazine with the headline, "NO. 1 ON T.V." The three on the cover of NEWSWEEK with the headline, "AMERICA'S FAVORITE!" Each photo in drag.*)

In addition to being the favorite comedy show in America, "Hello, Fellas" is also number one in Japan!

(PROJECTIONS: *Sony offices, Mitsubishi, Nissan, Emperor Hirohito, sumo wrestlers, samurai warriors, other Japanese images.*)

(PROJECTION: *TED, PHIL and KENNY on the covers of TIME*

and NEWSWEEK with Japanese lettering, wearing Kimono drag.)

TED, PHIL & KENNY. (*on backstage mikes*)
TOKYO IS A SCALY PRACE
ARWAYS ON THE GO
AH SO! IN TOKYO
WE CAN SAY WE GRAD TO MEET YA OOUGH!
HITE! HITE! HITE! HERRO FERRAS!

(PROJECTIONS *of Poland, the Gdansk Shipyard, Lech Walesa, the Pope.*)

TED. (*voiceover*) When they're not resisting the communist government, dockworkers in Poland watch the one T.V. show that has been allowed to slip through the Iron Curtain. And Lech Walesa himself came to see "Hello, Fellas" live at the Gdansk Shipyard!

(*Throughout the following verse, we see* PROJECTIONS *of TED, PHIL and KENNY on the covers of Polish magazines wearing babushka drag.*)

TED, PHIL & KENNY.(*on backstage mikes*)
HEY! PSHAW! IN WARSAW!
CAN WE SAY THE COP IS ZANY? HEY!
DA, DA, DA, CHELLO BOYCHICKS! HEY!

TED. (*voiceover*) Our favorite funnymen, Ted, Phil and Kenny, certainly showed the French that they "can-can" at the Lido de Paris!

(PROJECTIONS *of Eiffel Tower, covers of French magazines, Paris Match, Oui, in French drag.*)

TED. (*voiceover*) They had the camels holding their humps in Afghanistan!

(PROJECTIONS *of covers of Afghanistan magazines, posing in Afghanistani drag.*)

TED. (*voiceover*) And the Brazilians went bananas down in Rio de Janeiro!

(PROJECTIONS: *covers of South American magazines showing the guys posing in Carmen Miranda drag.*)

TED. (*voiceover*) And now! Following their record-breaking standing room only whirlwind tour of 18 countries around the world, we are happy to welcome home "Hello, Fellas" live at the M.G.M. Grand Hotel!

(*During the above, we see a* PROJECTION *of a map of the world with a line tracing their route. Then a* PROJECTION *of an honor guard giving a 21-gun salute. TED, PHIL and KENNY, in All-American drag, on the cover of Life magazine with the huge headline, "THEY'RE BACK!!" Various* PROJECTIONS *of the Vegas strip and M.G.M. Grand Hotel marquee.*)

(*Vegas music. Ribbon curtain drops. Smoke. Stair unit comes out.*)

(*LIVE: TED, PHIL, and KENNY come into view sitting on the stair unit that comes rolling with flashing chaser lights and border lights. They are wearing gorgeous red, white, and blue sequined gowns. They sing.*)

TED, PHIL & KENNY.
VEGAS IS A SCARY PLACE
DETECTIVES OUGHTA KNOW
THEY WORK AT SUCH A HARRIED PACE
THEY'RE ALWAYS ON THE GO
WHAT A GAS! IN VE-GAS!
WE CAN SAY WE'RE GLAD TO MEET YA!
(*spoken*) Good to see ya! (*sing*)
SURE COULD USE THREE ZANY COPS LIKE YOU . . .
OOH OOH OOH
OOH HOO HOO HOO HOO HOO HOO HOO HOO
OOH OOH OOH
HELLO FELLAS!!
DOO DWAH DOO DWAH DOO DWAH!

(*Stair unit rolls back and disappears as ribbon curtain closes*

*in front of it after TED, PHIL, and KENNY have stepped
onto the band platform above. DRUMBEAT kicks in im-
mediately.)*

[MUSIC #20A: DEMEANING]

(PROJECTIONS *of dressing room doors with stars that say "TED,"
"PHIL," and "KENNY." Lights change. TED, PHIL, and
KENNY take off their wigs and help each other out of their
gowns. The backstage dressing room set rolls on complete
with three lighted mirrors and stools. TED, PHIL and
KENNY walk down the stairs and onto the dressing room
area. The following goes in and out of rhythmic patter.)*

PHIL.
IT'S DEMEANING!
        TED.
YEP
    PHIL.
IT'S DEGRADING
        TED.
YO
    PHIL.
IT'S DEBASING
        TED.
YAHA
    PHIL.
AND IT'S DE STUPIDEST WAY TO TRY TO LIVE YOUR
        LIFE
        TED.
IT SUPPORTS YOUR WIFE AND THE LITTLE ONE TOO
WHEN'S IT DUE?
    PHIL.
ANY DAY
        TED.
ANY DAY?
    PHIL.
ANY DAY
        TED. O.K., so the timing's perfect. Your wife had three
months without you there to drive her crazy, and you got to see
the world as a woman for the first time.
    PHIL. And the last.

TED. Come on, Phil. (*rhythmic patter again*)
THIS IS JUST THE BEGINNING
WE CAN'T LEAVE THE TABLE
CUZ WE'RE HOT AND WE'RE WINNING
  PHIL.
WINNING WHAT, TED?
  KENNY.
IT
  TED.
MONEY
  KENNY.
DEBASEMENT
  TED.
MONEY
  PHIL.
IT'S DEMEANING!
  TED.
IT's DE MONEY!

PHIL. Hey Ted, come on. We didn't become a team just so we could make some bucks, cuz you know damn well if that's what I wanted I could've—

TED. All right! Whoa! Wait a minute! Relax! We all want the same thing. Look I know you're upset because you haven't seen your woman in a while but, hey,
IT'LL BE ALL RIGHT YOUR DOMESTIC SCENE
YOU JUST GOTTA KEEP SIGHT OF WHAT ALL THIS
  MEANS
  PHIL.
WHAT'S IT MEAN?
  TED.
WHAT'S IT MEAN!

KENNY. What's it mean? I'll tell you what it means. It means we're never going home. Ever again. So just click your heels three times and say (*Wicked Witch:*) I'm bleeding . . . bleeding . . . What a world . . . what a world . . . aah . . .

PHIL. He's losing it.

TED. He's okay.

PHIL. No he's not. Look at him. He's not O.K.

TED. Look Phil, don't tell me about Kenny.

PHIL. All right. (*makes sure KENNY's O.K.*) O.K. I'll speak for myself. I've had it, man. I'm not gonna do this bullshit anymore. I mean if you guys wanna keep on doing this "Hello,

Fellas" crap, that's just fine with me, but I'm not gonna do it!

TED. All right. Hold it! Just cool it for a second. First and foremost, we've got to stick together. No matter what. It's the team that counts. Right? And so far everything is going according to plan.

PHIL. Oh yeah? Whose plan?

TED. Our plan. And our agents, who at this very moment happen to be negotiating a movie deal with MGM.

PHIL & KENNY. *Wwwwwwhat?*

TED. That's right.

PHIL. Our own feature film?

TED. A "Hello, Fellas" feature film.

PHIL. "Hello, Fellas?!" Forget it man, no way!

TED. Whaddya mean, forget it?

KENNY. I have to go.

TED. What are you talking about?

PHIL. Let him go.

TED. (*to PHIL*) Are you out of your mind?

KENNY. I'm out of my mind! (*KENNY starts to leave.*)

TED. Will you cut it out!

PHIL. Hey, easy. Easy.

TED. So it's come to this huh? Phil Kunin telling me to calm down. And my best friend is walking out.

PHIL. All right Ted. You're right. We gotta stick together. But look, you gotta convince these movie people to let us do this film with our own material.

TED. Oh yeah? O.K. And what if they don't go for it?

PHIL. Then we don't go for it.

TED. We're not ready to . . .

PHIL. Ted, we're ready, man. That's why we came out here.

TED. Our own material?

PHIL. Yeah.

TED. I don't know man.

PHIL. TED . . . GUYS . . . COME ON . . . (*In rhythm*)
YOU WANNA BE A TEAM
YOU WANNA LIVE A DREAM
YOU WANNA TOUCH OF FAME
YOU WANNA STAKE A CLAIM
WELL LOOK:
THE TIME TO STRIKE IS NOW
IF WE DO THIS FLICK
IT'LL SHOCK AND SURPRISE

AND FOLKS ARE GONNA SAY
"WHO THE HELL ARE THESE GUYS?"
    TED.
THAT'S WHAT I'M AFRAID OF.
    PHIL.
TED,
COME ON
WE CAN PULL IT OFF
    TED.
IF WE DO IT RIGHT
    PHIL.
WE'LL DO IT RIGHT
CUZ WE'RE GATHERING MOMENTUM
(*Roller coaster* PROJECTIONS. *Dressing room set disappears*
    through ribbon curtain.)
AND GAINING SPEED
DON'T THINK OF WHAT
    CAN STOP US
JUST THINK OF WHAT
    WE NEED   TED.
DON'T THINK OF WHAT   CUZ WE'RE GATHERING
    CAN STOP US   MOMENTUM
JUST THINK OF WHAT WE   WE RUSH ALONG
    NEED
DON'T THINK OF WHAT   JUST THINK OF WHAT
    CAN STOP US   GOES RIGHT FOR US
JUST THINK OF WHAT WE   IF NOTHING CAN GO
    NEED   WRONG . . .

WHAT CAN GO WRONG?
    TED.
WHAT DO WE NEED?
    PHIL.
WE'RE GAINING SPEED
    TED.
WHAT CAN GO WRONG?

[MUSIC #21: LIGHTNING FLASHING/TWISTING LOCOMOTION]

    PHIL.
LET'S MOVE AHEAD!

TED, PHIL & KENNY. (*They put sunglasses on and sing.*)
RIDING THE CREST
SO HIGH AND FREE
FLUSHED WITH SUCCESS
IS ALL YOU WANT TO BE

TWISTING LOCOMOTION
HEAD AND STOMACH CHURNING
EYES AND EARS ARE BURNING
YOU WON'T RETURN
WITH A BRAIN THAT'S SOUND
WHAT A RIDE (*Fugue*)
WHAT A—

(*TED and KENNY keep sunglasses on.* PROJECTIONS: *City Lights. Joke Factory logo.*
We are now in THE JOKE FACTORY, another L.A. comedy club. MUSIC under. PHIL takes his sunglasses off. He is in the middle of his stand-up.)

PHIL. So there I am, in the middle of this meeting at MGM for the new movie, and the producers are giving us a bad time. So Kenny gets up on top of the conference table, starts doing tropical bird calls and flies out of the room. Ted tries to cover up for him and says "It's just a bit for the movie," but the producers call Kenny a 'psycho,' and threaten to cancel the project. O.K., so I pulled out my baseball bat and I was just about ready to shatter their sex lives when I get a call from my wife. She's about to have the baby. O.K., so I rush to the hospital, and I finally locate the birthing room, and there's my wife: screaming for drugs. I said, "Hey, show a little sensitivity for newborn life." And together we did a natural childbirth delivery without a hitch. (*MUSIC out.*) Y'know how everybody says newborn babies are so cute. I gotta tell ya, after several hours of shmushing your face up against a very small opening (*Shmushes his face*) and then trying to breathe for the first time in your life: (*smack, breathe, cry*) you newborn babies look like shit. But I gotta tell ya: my son was gorgeous.

[MUSIC #22: MIRROR/EXECUTION/SON]

TED. (*sings*)
WHAT A RIDE!

(*TED reaches for KENNY, who pulls away and leaves. TED moves* us. *into the darkness.*)

(PROJECTIONS: *Street at night in the rain*)

PHIL.
HELPLESS AND CONFUSED
FINGERS TOUCHING YOU
NO MORE FEAR
YOUR DADDY'S HERE
TO LOOK AT YOU . . .

The following optional song may be done at this point:

[MUSIC #22½: A FATHER NOW]

PHIL.
I'M A FATHER NOW
THAT'S WHAT I ALWAYS WANTED
TO HAVE A LITTLE BOY TO DO THINGS FOR
A FAMILY NOW
THAT'S WHAT I ALWAYS WANTED
A WIFE A SON
WHO I COULD FIGHT FOR
THIS IS WHAT I'VE ALWAYS NEEDED
TO BE THE ONE WHO THEY CAN TRUST
AND WHEN I THINK OF ME
NOW I'LL HAVE TO THINK OF US

I'M A FATHER NOW
THAT'S WHAT I ALWAYS WANTED
HAVE THE MONEY TO BUILD A HOME
A FAMILY NOW
THAT'S WHAT I ALWAYS WANTED
WHEN I FACE THE WORLD
I WON'T HAVE TO FACE IT ALONE
THIS IS WHAT I'VE ALWAYS NEEDED

TO SEE MYSELF IN MY SON'S EYES
SO HE'LL KNOW I'M ON HIS SIDE
HE WON'T HAVE TO TELL ME LIES

WANT MY BOY TO LOOK UP TO ME
EMULATE ME NOT JUST IMITATE ME
IT'S TIME TO ANSWER QUESTIONS
AND MAKE SOME FAST DECISIONS
THAT I CAN LIVE WITH
SO I CAN LIVE WITH MYSELF

SO BE A FATHER NOW
AND BE WHAT YOU'VE ALWAYS WANTED
SCORE SOME POINTS YOU CAN SHOW WITH PRIDE
A FAMILY NOW
MAY BE WHAT YOU'VE ALWAYS WANTED
BUT YOU HAVE SO MUCH TO SAY
THAT YOU'VE KEPT INSIDE
GO FOR WHAT YOU'VE ALWAYS NEEDED
RISK YOUR WORK BUT NOT YOUR HOME
AND WHEN YOU LOOK IN YOUR SON'S EYES
YOU WON'T TELL EACH OTHER LIES
AND IF YOU'VE SUCCEEDED
YOU'LL KNOW

(*Lights dim to black on PHIL. Lights up on TED. He stands before an imaginary mirror.*)

TED. (*sings*)
I GOT ME A MIRROR I LOOKED AT MY FACE AND SAID WOW!
Someday you're gonna be on your own pal . . . And the year was 1999! And "Hello Fellas" was still the number one show on television! But then, Phil Kunin decided to run for President of the United States! Kenny Brewster founded the Zen Catholic Big Brothers, and it appeared that the series would have to be cancelled! Until one man! One very silly man! Convinced the network he could play all three roles himself! Ladies and gentlemen, TED KLAUSTERMAN!! Give me a break, Ted.

(*Lights up on KENNY, sitting on the edge of the band platform.*

He is placing a noose around his dummy, STEVE's neck, just as he did with "Hall of Martyrs" in Act I.)

STEVE. Hey, what're you doing? I don't need a necktie. (*KENNY presses the play/record button on his tape recorder.*) What is this, some kind of joke? (*KENNY pulls the noose tight around STEVE's neck. STEVE chokes. KENNY holds the tape recorder closer.*) What's the matter? You think you're funny? (*chokes*) O.K. you're funny. See I'm laughing already. AAAUGH! (*KENNY hangs STEVE. Lights down on KENNY.*)

(*Lights up on TED.*)

TED. "Ernie," a musical rock opera about the life of Ernest Hemingway, written by, directed by, and starring Ted Klausterman. (*pause*) You better grow up, pal. (*Lights down on TED.*)

(*Lights up on KENNY.*)

STEVE. Go ahead. Chop my head off. You'll be better off without me.
KENNY. NO! I don't wanna be by myself, Steve. (*KENNY pulls out a gun and puts it to his head.*)
STEVE. Hey, put that thing away—
KENNY. I can't live without you, Steve.
STEVE. I'm not goin' anywhere. Put it away.
KENNY. Why don't you come with me? (*puts gun away*)
STEVE. Where we goin'?

(PROJECTION: *Variety, Hollywood Reporter, Dramalogue. Headlines read: "FELLAS PIC SKED FOR FEB" "HELLO FELLAS T.V. TO FILM" "COPS IN DRAG ON THE BIG SCREEN."*)

When the song "A FATHER NOW" is omitted, the following is done:

(*Lights up on PHIL.*)

[MUSIC #22¾: MIRROR PART II]

> PHIL. (*sings*)
> OUR VOICES GETTING SOFTER NOW
> CHILLS UP AND DOWN MY SPINE
> I FEEL THE JOY OF LIVING
> FROM HIS DANCING EYES TO MINE
> OUR HEARTS ARE FILLED WITH DREAMS
> OF PRAISES TO BE SUNG
> THE TIME FOR BETTER TIMES
> HAS COME
> MY SON . . .

(*Lights up on TED and PHIL.*)

TED. And now MGM presents: Ted Klausterman, Phil Kunin and Kenny Brewster in an exciting new feature film, "3 GUYS NAKED FROM THE WAIST DOWN."

[MUSIC #22A: FLASHIN' REPRISE]

(*TED sings and starts up the stage R. stairs.*)

FLASHIN' ON THE SCREEN
SHAKIN' IN OUR SHOES
STICKIN' TO OUR GUNS
  PHIL.
YEAH!

(*PHIL sings and starts up the stage L. stairs.*)

FLASHIN' ON THE—
SHAKING IN OUR—
STICKIN' TO OUR GUNS
  TED & PHIL.
YEAH!
FLASHIN'
SHAKIN'
STICKIN'
WHOA! YEAH! YEAH! YEAH!

(*Standing up high on the band platform, TED and PHIL lift*

KENNY up and they put on their sunglasses. PROJECTIONS: *Roller coasters*)

[MUSIC #23: MOTOR-POWERED]

TED, PHIL & KENNY. (*This was on prerecorded tape in the original production, but it can be done live if desired.*)
MOTOR POWERED MONSTER
PLUMMET FAST AND FASTER
LAUGHING AT DISASTER
    TED.
YOU'LL BE THE MASTER
    PHIL & KENNY.
YOU'LL BE THE MASTER
    TED, PHIL & KENNY.
IF YOU MAKE IT BACK
    PHIL.
WHAT A RIDE
    KENNY.
WHAT A RIDE
    TED.
WHAT A RIDE
    TED, PHIL & KENNY.
WHAT A RIDE

VOICEOVER. (& PROJECTION) This Preview has been approved for all audiences by the Motion Picture Association of America, rated PG-13

(PROJECTION *out.*)

[MUSIC #24: 3 GUYS NAKED]

(*Whistles, sirens, crashing sounds. TED and KENNY run on.*)

TED. Look out! Run for cover!
KENNY. *Aaaugh!*

(PROJECTIONS *of dark deserted cobblestone streets*)

TED & KENNY.
THERE'S TROUBLE ALL AROUND

DANGER LURKING EVERYWHERE
RUMBLING UNDERGROUND
AND PANIC IN THE STREETS
CAUSING TENSION IN THE AIR

(*PHIL jumps on. NEWS MUSIC under.* PROJECTION: *Hand with knife, center. City lights on side with "SPECIAL BULLETIN" superimposed.*)

PHIL. (*newsanchorman*) We interrupt this program to bring you this special news bulletin. The dreaded Nightclub Killer has just claimed his twenty-fourth victim. New York City continues to be terrorized by this crazed murderer who frequents late night cafes and cabarets and kills at random a member of the audience.

(*TED is joined by PHIL and KENNY in a comedy nightclub.*)

(PROJECTION: *Nightclub logo:* "LAUGHS Я US")

TED. Hi there. How ya doin'? Where ya from? (*KENNY lets out a death scream.*) Funny. I was just there last week. We're gonna do a little improv for you tonight, so let's bring the lights up and—Oh my God! Oh no! *He's struck again!*

(PROJECTION: *Dark deserted cobblestone streets*)

TED, PHIL & KENNY. (*sing*)
THERE'S PERIL HIGH AND LOW
COMPLICATIONS LEFT AND RIGHT
EVERYWHERE YOU GO
THERE'S TERROR IN YOUR HEART YOU'LL NEED HELP
TO WIN THE FIGHT

(PROJECTION: *Hand with knife, flanked by "SPECIAL BULLETIN"*)

PHIL. (*newsman in the street*) This just in. The dreaded Nightclub Killer has just been apprehended by three stand-up comics who, according to two eyewitnesses (*TED and KENNY babble hysterically.*)—what they're trying to say is the 3 stand-up comics surrounded the murderer and then took off their pants. This so surprised the homicidal maniac that he gladly gave himself

up. This is incredible! (*MUSIC fades. To TED and KENNY:*)
Do you think these three comedians can help catch The Midtown
Mangler? The Brownstone Butcher? The Soho Sniper? or the
Eastside Strangler?!

(*Police siren. They rip off their shirts, coats, and ties to reveal
    their "Naked Guys" logo T-shirts.*)

TED, PHIL & KENNY.
MANGLER! BUTCHER! SNIPER! STRANGLER!
MANGLER!-BUTCHER!-SNIPER!-STRANGLER!
(*sing, with white hats in hand*)
WHO'S GONNA DOUSE THAT FLAME
WHO'S GONNA BREAK THE ICE
KENNY.
SOMEONE'S GOT TO TAME THE BEAST
THAT'S GOT THE CITY LOCKED UP IN A VICE
TED.
LOOK
PHIL.
LOOK
TED, PHIL & KENNY.
LOOK AROUND
FOR THREE GUYS
THREE GUYS NAKED FROM THE WAIST DOWN

(PROJECTIONS: *newspaper headlines: NY Daily News, "NIGHT-
    MARE ENDED BY 3 CHEEKY CIVILIANS"; NY Post,
    "THEY'RE NAKED!"; NY Times, "NIGHTCLUB KILLER
    APPREHENDED".*)

PHIL. (*puts on sunglasses; Ridiculous Dick*) That's right! So
check your local movie listings because these 3 Naked Guys are
gonna be coming to your neighborhood!

(*During the following, TED, PHIL, and KENNY appear and
    disappear through the ribbon curtain.*)

KENNY. (*Syringe. LENNY:*) No, George, I don't want 3 Naked
Guys coming to my neighborhood! (*GEORGE:*) Lenny, you
better have 3 Naked Guys come to your neighborhood or I'll
turn you into an extra-terrestrial! (*LENNY:*) All right!
(*GEORGE:*) Too late! (*KENNY becomes E.T.:*) Elliott!

TED. As you can see COMEDY IS DANGEROUS! But at least you can turn to the person sitting next to you and say, "Sure, my life sucks, but at least I'm not in this movie."

KENNY. (*Mickey Mouse hat and Bullwhip:*) Shay Kidsh! You wanna see a great movie? (*Little Boy:*) Yeah, yeah, I wanna see a great movie! (*Rasping voice:*) C'mere. Pull down your pants and bend over! (*cracks the whip*)

TED. Sir! Please! He was just kidding! This is a movie for the whole family!

PHIL. (*Ridiculous Dick*) That's right. The whole family! And by Christmastime, the Naked Guy Craze will be catching on in the White House, The Forbidden City, and The Kremlin! WHAT!

(*Abstract* PROJECTION *of naked derriere in front of U.S. flag, then China flag, then Russian flag.*)

TED.
WHAT?!
KENNY.
WHAT?!
TED, PHIL & KENNY.
THAT'S RIGHT!

(PROJECTIONS: *magazine headlines: Newsweek, "THE BOYS IN THE BUFF!"; Life, "EVERYBODY'S DOIN' IT! "; Time, "NAKED NEGOTIATORS!"*)

WHO'S GONNA DOUSE, GONNA DOUSE THAT FLAME
3 GUYS
WHO'S GONNA BREAK BREAK BREAK THE ICE
3 GUYS NAKED
DANGER LURKS, TERROR STRIKES
WE GOTTA TAME THE BEAST
BREAK THE VICE
LOOK AROUND, LEFT AND RIGHT
HIGH AND LOW, WIN THE FIGHT
LOOK AROUND
(PROJECTION: *3 Guys logo*)
FOR 3 GUYS
3 GUYS NAKED
3 GUYS NAKED FROM THE WAIST . . .
(*Drumbreak. Lights out, Blacklights on.*)

3 GUYS NAKED FROM THE WAIST DOWN
(*Their overdressed, white pants, seen in blacklight, are ripped away in the dark, so we just see their white hats.*)

(*BLACKOUT*)

(PROJECTION: *City lights*)

VOICEOVER. And now just when you thought it was safe to "Go For Broke," The Komedy Klub West presents: Ted, Phil and Kenny in "Killer Critics"!

[MUSIC #25: KILLER CRITICS]

(*Lights up. THE KOMEDY KLUB WEST rolls on with TED, PHIL, and KENNY, standing with their backs to the audience. PHIL and TED turn around when they speak, while KENNY remains with his back to the audience.*)

PHIL. Doris Blunderhaus Channel 4, I just saw the "Hello, Fellas" boys feature film "3 Guys Naked From The Waist Down" and I must say, I didn't understand it.

TED. Nick Tittsenasskey Channel 2, I understood it, and I hated it.

KENNY. Bless me Father for I have sinned.

PHIL. (*Doris*) I was looking forward to a couple hours of frontal nudity.

TED. (*Nick*) I wasn't looking forward to it and I still hated it.

KENNY. Father, I deserted my friends.

TED. (*Gardner*) Listen boys, nobody's going to see the picture. We need publicity. But Brewster's not cooperating. Tell 'em Elliot.

PHIL. (*Ross*) Nobody's going to see the picture. Where's Brewster?

KENNY. Father I . . .

TED. (*Gardner*) Take it from me Boys. You're better off doing "Hello, Fellas" projects down the line. Tell 'em Elliot.

PHIL. (*Ross*) "Hello, Fellas" projects down the line.

TED. And Johnny Carson opened his monologue last night by saying "If you saw '3 Guys Naked From The Waist Down,' you got the short end of the stick."

PHIL. They didn't like us.

TED. "Hello, Fellas" projects down the line.

PHIL. They're making fun of us. (*MUSIC out.*)

TED. (*Gardner*) Listen Boys, you better reconsider. You can't just walk away from the number one show on television. Tell 'em Elliot.

PHIL. (*Ross*) You can't walk away.

TED. (*Gardner*) Cuz if you do, you're gonna have to start from scratch. Tell 'em Elliot.

PHIL. (*Ross*) Start from scratch.

TED. (*Gardner*) All right Boys, if that's your decision. But you're making a big mistake. Tell 'em Elliot.

PHIL. (*Ross*) A big mistake.

TED. (*Gardner*) Cuz nobody's gonna wanna touch you, you're gonna have to—

KENNY. SHHHHHHH!

[MUSIC #26: SUPER-DUMMIES]

(*TED, PHIL and KENNY step around, revealing their dummies sitting on stools. They stand behind their dummies working their mouths.*)

(PROJECTION: *Dummies' faces superimposed over city lights.*)

STEVE.
HEY CATS
THE CLOCKS ARE SCREAMING IN THE NIGHT

PHIL. Where the Hell is Kenny?

TED. He's gone.

STEVE.
HEY CATS,
LISTEN TIGHT FOR THE NEXT URBAN EXPLOSION

PHIL. What are we gonna do?

TED. I don't know. I've just got to get out of here.

STEVE.
ON SUPER VICIOUS CYCLE BREAKING VISTAS

PHIL. Where are you gonna go?

TED. Back to New York.

PHIL. Why New York?

TED. I think Kenny might be back there.

PHIL. O.K. Great. You bring him back, man. The three of us have got a lot of things to do.

MR. DIRTBALL, SPIKE, STEVE.
WE'RE THE NEXT GENERATION OF HEROES

TED. Look Phil, you might have to face the fact that it's over, man.

PHIL. Ted, no! Look, don't worry, you'll find him.

MR. DIRTBALL. Look, guys.
IF YOU PULL YOUR SHIT TOGETHER
SPIKE.
AND YOU WATCH YOUR FUCKING LANGUAGE
DIRTBALL & SPIKE.
AND YOU MAKE YOUR CRAP ACCESSIBLE
STEVE.
THE NEXT THING YOU KNOW . . .

TED.
NO!
PHIL.
NO!
KENNY.
NO!
TED.
DON'T WANNA BE NO—

PHIL.
LAUGHING AT DISASTER
YOU'LL BE THE MASTER
IF YOU MAKE IT BACK
WHAT A RIDE, WHAT A RIDE,
WHAT A RIDE, WHAT A RIDE . . .
WHAT A RIDE, WHAT A RIDE,
WHAT A RIDE, WHAT A RIDE . . .
TED.
DON'T WANNA BE A SUPERSTAR

(*TED and PHIL are pulled off with the set; KENNY is alone.*)

[MUSIC #27: DREAM REPRISE]

(PROJECTION: *cluster of stars, nebulae*)

KENNY.
IT TOOK EACH NIGHT TO GET HERE
NOW MY SOUL IS ALL ABLAZE
IT'S AGONY TO HAVE TO KISS THIS LIFE GOOD BYE
BUT I'LL TRY
DREAMS OF HEAVEN
WILL HELP ME

(*KENNY slowly walks off leaving STEVE. TED comes on,
sees the abandoned dummy. He knows KENNY has killed
himself. TED picks the dummy up, and sets it down carefully
on the piano, as if it were KENNY's body. He sits for a
moment, then starts to tinker at the piano.*)

[MUSIC #28: HEROES]

(PROJECTION: *L.A. city lights*)

TED. (*sings*)
WHEN I WAS A LITTLE KID
ROBIN HOOD PATROLLED THE WOOD
WITH FEATS TOO BRAVE AND DARING TO BELIEVE
AND IN THE DARK OF SUMMER NIGHTS
SIR GALAHAD WAS ALL I HAD
TO SHOW WHAT STRENGTH AND PURITY SHOULD BE
THE HEROES I READ ABOUT
WERE WHAT A MAN SHOULD BE
THE HEROES I DREAMED ABOUT
WERE ALL REPLACED BY ME
I FOUGHT THE VILLAINS SAVED THE MAIDS
AND TURNED THE TIDE OF WAR
BUT NOW I'M ALL GROWN UP
I DON'T BELIEVE IN HEROES ANYMORE

WHEN I WAS A BOY OF TEN
J.F.K. HAD SHOWN THE WAY
TO PUSH THE RUSSIANS BACK FROM FIRING RANGE
AND IN MY TEENS A MAN CALLED "CHE"

SPREAD WORD OF MARX AND MAO TO SAY
THE WORLD MUST CHANGE
THROUGH HARSH AND VIOLENT MEANS
I SAT BEFORE MY T.V. SET
AND WATCHED MY HEROES DIE
I READ THE RAGS AND PAPERS
SHOWING PROOF MY HEROES LIED
WITH EARLY DEATH THEIR ONLY WREATH
TO PASS THROUGH HEAVEN'S DOOR
I SEE THEIR CONTRADICTIONS
AND I DON'T BELIEVE IN HEROES ANYMORE

(PROJECTION: *Brooklyn Bridge (*L. & R.*). Statue of Liberty (*C.*)*)

OHHHHHH . . .
TO JUST BE NAIVE
TO LIVE IN A DREAM
TO HAVE SOMEONE TO BELIEVE
OHHHHHH . . .
WHY CAN'T LIFE BE CLEAN
TO JUST WIN ONE FOR THE TEAM
IT'S NOT AS SIMPLE AS IT SEEMS

(PROJECTION: *"Klausterman's" logo, superimposed over Statue of Liberty*)

WHEN I LEFT THE COLLEGE SCENE
WE'D MADE OUR PEACE OUT IN THE EAST
AND SCRATCHED THE COUNTLESS DEAD ON
    POLISHED WALLS
AND NOW I HEAR THE COUNTRY CRY
FOR GOOD OLD DAYS WHEN FLAGS WERE RAISED
AND GOD WAS ON OUR SIDE AGAINST THEM ALL
I WONDER WHY
THE HEROES WE CLAMOR FOR
ARE MEN FROM PAST ROMANCE
THE HEROES WE GATHER FOR
PERFORM A PUPPET'S DANCE
WE'RE FOOLS IF WE CAN'T SEE THE FOOLS
WHO'VE FOOLED US ALL BEFORE
EXCEPT WHEN I READ BOOKS AND DREAM
I DON'T BELIEVE IN HEROES
ANYMORE

(*Lights change. We are now in "KLAUSTERMAN'S," TED's Comedy Club.*)

TED. (*continued*) O.K., Ladies and Gentlemen, we're having some show here tonight and that's how it is every night here at "Klausterman's." The place where you can sit back, relax, and watch young stand-up comics get up on stage and make good money by pondering the universe. I know what you're thinking. You're saying to yourselves, "Say Ted, you used to be a real successful guy. Money. Fame. Designer Gowns. And now God Bless you, you're an M.C. again. Where'd you Fuck Up? Well, I guess that depends on how you look at it. I mean, success is funny. It doesn't really exist. We just pretend it does so we know how much money to hide from the government. You know, speaking of success, the number one show on television right now is about a C.I.A. agent who works undercover . . . in Russia . . . in drag. It's called "Hello, Comrade," starring Phil Kunin. Phil's wife just had another baby and he sent me a picture of himself sitting in the bathtub with his two little boys. And in the picture all three of them are holding little rubber baseball bats. Underneath it he wrote, "Three Naked Angry Guys." It's tough when you hardly get to see a good buddy anymore. About six months ago, another good buddy of mine, Kenny Brewster, decided to check out the comedy circuit in eternity. And knowing Kenny, well, he's probably up there breaking in on everybody else's act and getting big laughs from that great M.C. in the sky. As for me, well, I'm a deep guy, and you're a deep crowd, and this is a deep band. How about these guys? Aren't they something? (*Name of the MUSICAL DIRECTOR*), my musical director and I go way back. When was the first time we played together? (*MUSICAL DIRECTOR ad libs. Example:* "When you sang 'My Way' at the Miller Lite Celebrity Wife Swapping Competition.") (*TED ad libs response. Example:* "This is coming from a man who has sexual fantasies about the Statue of Liberty.") Before we continue I think we should all savor this moment: (*pause*) . . . and now this moment: (*pause*) . . . and now let's savor the memory of those two moments: (*pause*) . . . A 5, 6, 7, 8 — [MUSIC #29: PROMISE FINALE] (*sings*)
I GOT THE PROMISE OF GREATNESS
THAT'S SOMETHING I JUST GOTTA SAY
NO MATTER WHAT COMES UP OR KNOCKS ME DOWN
I KNOW I'LL BE O.K.

CUZ I GOT
PROMISE OF GREATNESS
BU DAP DAP
I'M A HELLUVA GUY
BU DAP BU DAP BUBU DABA DA DOW
I GOT ME A NIGHT CLUB
I GOT ME A CROWD
AND HEY, I GOT ME A PLACE TO PLAY . . .

CUZ AIN' LIFE A BITCH
AIN'T LIFE A BITCH
AIN'T LIFE A BITCH—
All right, Ladies and Gentlemen, the man you are about to meet is an exciting newcomer to the comedy scene. This is his first appearance here at Klausterman's, so let's have a big hand for Danny Phillips.

(*TED starts the applause. Lights fade out on TED.*)

BLACKOUT

[MUSIC #30: BOWS/EXIT]

THE END

PROP LIST

3 Ventriloquist dummies (Steve, Spike, & Mr. Dirtball)
2 Short stools — for airplane scene
3 Tall stools
1 Mic — not functional
Small tape recorder
Bullwhip
Mickey Mouse Ears
Vogue face
Syringe
Stuffed cat
Phone receiver
Apple
Neutral mask
Zombie ball
Silver bag
Small plastic axe
Gun
Noose for dummy's head
Black hood (For Kenny)
Tall beer can (empty)
Blue spike tape
Newspaper — mocked up with "Angry Guy" headline
Basketball
Guitar
Harmonica
2 Airline oxygen masks
2 Emergency airline pamphlets
2 Airline seat belts
2 Airsickness bags
An empty champagne bottle
3 Flier goggles
3 Pair sunglasses
1 Standard contract
Character glasses: Elliot, Dick, Lance, Bobby Bud
Pipe
Grey hat (fedora)
Kids hat
Ghetto blaster
6 Pack of beer
3 Scripts

3 Dowels (t make dummies sit up on stools)
1 Cigar
1 Pair sunglasses: Ridiculous Dick

COSTUME BREAKDOWN

TED

ACT I

Basic (Constant):
    Grey socks with red tops
    Charcoal grey checked trousers with grey suspenders
"Stand-Up":
    Tweed jacket, sleeves tacked up to 3/4 length
    "Who Me?" T-shirt
    Black sneakers, white laces
"Dummies":
    Red sneakers, white elastic laces
"History of Stand-Up":
    Admiral's coat with medals and braid
    Bicorn hat with feathers
"Columbus Circle":
    Kneepads
    Same tweed jacket
    Plain white T-shirt

ACT II

Basic (Constant):
    Grey socks with red tops
    Kneepads
    Maroon sneakers, maroon elastic laces
"American Dream"
    Turquoise print boxer shorts
    Dark grey breakaway pants, purple stripes
    Turquoise print shirt, sleeveless
    Detached collar for shirt
    Black tie, attached to collar by velcro
    Dark green sharkskin jacket, black pocket triangle
    Mexican vest
    White dinner jacket
"Agents #1":
    Grey Hawaiian shirt
    Light blue shorts
    Sunglasses (prop)

93

"Agents #2":
   White jacket with pastel stripes
   Black flowered shirt, pinned into jacket
   White pants, beige vertical stripes
   Grey fedora (prop)
"Vegas":
   Silver sequin dress
   Blonde wig
"Mirrors":
   Grey jacket, gold dots
   Green/black sleeveless shirt
   Black "3 Guys" T-shirt
   Black trousers
   Sunglasses (prop)
"Movie":
   Grey jacket with pocket handkerchief that matches dickie
   Dickie with bow tie
   White breakaway pants
   White hat
   Sunglasses (prop)
"Heroes":
   Repeat grey jacket, gold dots
   Green print corduroy shirt
   Repeat black trousers

PHIL

ACT I

Basic (Constant):
   Cream colored socks/red tops
   Grey sneakers, black elastic laces
   Light khaki chinos, green web belt
   Mauve/grey plaid shirt
"Stand-Up":
   Grey baseball jacket
"History of Stand-up":
   Green pirates coat
   Black pirates hat with flag

ACT II

Basic (Constant):

Cream colored socks/red tops
Grey sneakers, black elastic laces
"American Dream":
  Polka dot boxer shorts
  Purple breakaway trousers
  Blue/brown/black sleeveless shirt
  Detached collar for shirt
  Rose tie attached to collar by pin
  Red sharkskin jacket
  Bluejean jacket with fur collar
  "Dylan" wig
  White dinner jacket
"Agents #1":
  White print Hawaiian shirt
  Dark blue shorts
  Sunglasses (prop)
"Agents #2":
  Light grey brushed denim pants
  Short sleeve Mexican shirt
  "Riddie Dick" glasses (prop)
"Vegas":
  Blue sequin dress
  Curly dark wig
"Mirrors":
  Black pants
  Rugby shirt
  Black "3 Guys" T-shirt
  Sunglasses (prop)
"Movie":
  Grey jacket with pocket handkerchief
  Dickie with attached bow tie
  White breakaway pants
  White hat
  Sunglasses (prop)

KENNY

ACT I

Basic (Constant):
  Kneepads
  Black sneakers

Orange socks
Blue T-shirt, sleeveless and cut down at neck
"Hall of Martyrs"
  #1 Monk:
Long Monk's robe
Monk's hood
Wide black leather belt
  #2 St. Sebastian:
Blue open weave tunic with arrows
Rope belt
  #3 Headless Man:
Heavy canvas jumpsuit
Padded and upholstered football shoulderpad head-piece
"Stand-Up":
Khaki pants, tan web belt
Rust shirt, sleeves tacked up to 3/4 length
Blue down coat with false padded arm sewn into pocket
"History of Stand-Up":
Oriental headband
Short oriental kimono

ACT II

Basic (Constant)
Kneepads
Black sneakers
White socks
"American Dream":
Plaid boxer shorts
Turquoise/black striped breakaway pants
Red/black checked sleeveless shirt
Detached collar for shirt
Purple tie attached to collar by safety pin
Light green sharkskin jacket
Suede fringed vest
White dinner jacket, rhinestone "?" pin on left lapel
"Agents #1":
Peach Hawaiian shirt
Khaki brown shorts
Sunglasses (prop)
Yellow handkerchief

"Agents #2":
  Blue pullover
  Charcoal pants
"Vegas":
  Red sequin dress
  Brown pageboy wig
"Mirrors":
  Leather shorts
  Black "3 Guys" T-shirt
  Punk Rocker face T-shirt
  Bandanas (2 sewn together)
  Sunglasses (prop)
"Mirror-Execution"
  Leather handguard
  "Rat Poison" leather vest with plaid shirt sewn inside
  Tote bag (prop)
"Movie":
  Grey jacket with pocket handkerchief
  Dickie with attached bow tie
  White breakaway pants
  White hat
  Sunglasses (prop)

PROPS AND COSTUMES

PRESET CHECKLIST

ACT I

Dressing Room:

KENNY:
Black sneakers
Orange socks
Kneepads
Blue T-shirt
Monk's robe and hood
Black leather belt for Monk's robe

PHIL:
Grey sneakers
Cream socks with red tops
Light khaki trousers, green web belt
Mauve/grey plaid shirt
Grey baseball jacket, orange trim

TED:
Black sneakers
Red sneakers
Grey socks with red tops
Charcoal checked trousers with grey suspenders
"Who Me?" T-shirt
Tweed jacket

Stage Right:

KENNY:
St. Sebastian tunic with rope belt

TED:
Plain T-shirt
Kneepads
Water bottle
Prop-table:
3 Flight scarves

Stage Left:

KENNY
Blue down coat
Headless man jumpsuit and shoulderpads
Oriental headband
Short oriental kimono
*Head
*Hatchet
*"Steve"
*White face mask
*Silver bag with revolver, black executioner's hood, and noose
*6-shooter
*White glove
*Apple
*Telephone receiver with cord
*Bic lighter
*Cigarette
Water bottle

PHIL:
Green Pirate's coat
Pirate's hat

TED:
Admiral's coat
Admiral's bicorn hat

ACT II

Dressing Room:

KENNY:
Black sneakers (from Act I)
Kneepads
White socks
Plaid boxer shorts
Turquoise/black stripe breakaway pants
Red/black checked sleeveless shirt
Detached collar for shirt with purple tie
Green sharkskin jacket

(*props)

PHIL:
Grey sneakers (from Act I)
Cream socks with red tops (from Act I)
Polka dot boxer shorts
Purple breakaway trousers
Blue/black/brown sleeveless shirt
Detached collar for shirt with rose tie
Red sharkskin jacket

TED:
Maroon sneakers
Grey socks with red tops (from Act I)
Dark grey breakaway trousers with purple stripes
Turquoise chambray sleeveless shirt
Detached collar for shirt with black tie
Dark green sharkskin jacket

Stage Left:

KENNY:
Fringe leather vest
White dinner jacket, rhinestone "?" pin
Peach Hawaiian shirt
Brown khaki shorts with pink handkerchief in R. front pocket
Blue pullover
Charcoal pants
Red sequin dress
Brown pageboy wig
Punk Face T-shirt
Black "3-Guys" T-shirt
Leather shorts
Bandanas
Leather vest with sewn-in plaid shirt
Leather handguard
Grey movie jacket
Dickie with attached bow tie
White breakaway pants
White hat
*Sunglasses
*Steve

_____

(*props)

*Tape recorder
*Water bottle

PHIL:
Denim jacket, fur collar
"Dylan" wig
White dinner jacket
White Hawaiian shirt
Dark blue shorts
Light green brushed denim pants
Mexican shirt
Blue sequin dress
Curly dark wig
Black pants
Rugby shirt
Black "3-Guys" T-shirt
Grey movie jacket
Dickie with attached bow tie
White breakaway pants
White hat
*Sunglasses
*Riddie Dick glasses
*Water bottle

TED:
Mexican Vest
White dinner jacket
Grey Hawaiian shirt
Light blue shorts
White jacket with pastel stripes and black floral shirt
    pinned into it
White pants with beige vertical stripes
Silver sequin dress
Blonde wig
Grey jacket, gold dots
Green/black sleeveless shirt
Black "3-Guys" T-shirt
Black pants
Grey movie jacket
Movie dickie with attached bow tie
White breakaway pants

(*props)

White hat
Green corduroy shirt
*Sunglasses
*Water bottle

(*props)

SLIDE ORDER LISTING

ACT I

CUE #	PAGE #	DESCRIPTION
0	0	Preset: Filtered light (black slide with spot-light effect)
2	9	Fade to Black (in overture) (BLACKOUT)
3	9	(c.s.) Reagan and Nancy (s.l. & s.r.) Flags
4	9	(s.l.) Reagan (c.s.) Map (s.r.) Soviet Man
5	9	(s.l.) Ford (c.s.) Carter (s.r.) Nixon
6	9	(c.s.) Mondale (s.l. & s.r.) Flags
7	9	Montage to 3 Reagan photos to Blackout
8	10	(c.s.) Ted (s.r. & s.l.) City Lights
9	10	City lights all 3 screens
10	10	Add "Komedy Klub East" to c.s. Screen
11	18	Painted brick walls (Street, alley)
12	21	City lights All screens
13	22	Add "Last Stand Up" c.s
14	30	"Last Stand Up" fades out
15	34	New City lights up
16	36	Add "Funny Farm" c.s.
17	41	"Funny Farm" fades, Nebula up all screens
18	42	All screens fade to black
19	42	Night in Central Park
20/21	47	Night fade. Airport sequence into Clouds up
21B	48	"Final Boarding" and "No Smoking" flash on and off
22	51	3 Guys free-falling up

ACT II

CUE #	PAGE #	DESCRIPTION
23	52	Preset out
24	52	Churchill, Ike & Kruschev
25	52	Maps up to (s.l.) IKE (c.s.) Map (s.r.) Kruschev
26	52	House, Glasses Davey Crocket
27	52	JFK, Marilyn Monroe, Elvis
28	52	Collage with 3 Ikes
29	52	3 Guys baby shots

103

ACT II (continued)

CUE #	PAGE #	DESCRIPTION
30	53	3 Guys baby shots with "Who Me"
31	53	3 Guys 1950's shots
32	54	3 Guys 1960's shots
33	55	3 Guys 1970's shots
34	56	Flags all screens
35	57	(s.l.) Mt. Rushmore (s.r.) Iwo Jima (c.s.) "Who Me"
36	57	Crowds up all screens
37	57	Crowds with glasses added
38	58	First Rollercoaster
39	58	L.A. Lights all screens (c.s.) "Komedy Klub West"
40	60	"Komedy Klub West" out, street projections in
41	63	Second Rollercoaster sequence
42	63	"Rehearsal" sign into Prism Lights
43	65	Flashing "On the Air" sign
44	65	No slide—black
45	65	NBC slide into "Hello Fellas" logo
45-65	65	"Hello, Fellas" sequence
66	66	City lights all screens (c.s.) "Comic Retreat"
67-76	68-70	"Hello, Fellas" World Tour (see text of play for exact sequence) into "$" signs
77	70	"MGM GRAND" logo
78	71	3 Guys "Stars"
79	74	Third Rollercoaster sequence
80	75	Lights (c.s.) Joke Factory
81	76	Rainbow lights (city lights)
82	77	Stripe lights
83	78	*Variety, Hollywood, The Register* Magazines
84	80	Fourth Rollercoaster sequence
85-90		Cut/—
91	80	"P.G. 13" slide
92	80	Fade to Black
93	80	Brick street shots (c.s.) Car
94	81	Lights (s.r. & s.l.) (c.s.) Hand with knife
95	81	"Laughs Я Us" sign
96	81	Crime in the streets & street slides
97	81	(c.s.) "Killer" (s.l. & s.r.) Lights

ACT II (continued)

CUE #	PAGE #	DESCRIPTION
98	—	—
99	—	—
100	82	(c.s.) Black (s.r. & s.l.) Twin posts
101	—	—
102	83	Flags with Derieres superimposed (s.r.) USSR (c.s.) China (s.l.) USA
103	83	Life, Time, Newsweek
104	83	"3 Guys" logo
105	84	Lights & (c.s.) "Komedy Klub West"
106	85	"Komedy Klub West" out, Dummies over Lights in
107	87	Nebula
108	87	Nebula out
109	87	L.A. Lights
110	88	(s.r. & s.l.) Bridges (c.s.) Statue of Liberty
111	88	"Klausterman's" sign (c.s.)
112	90	NYC cross fade to black
113	90	Curtain Call, Lights
114	90	Fade to Black
115	90	Post show, Lights

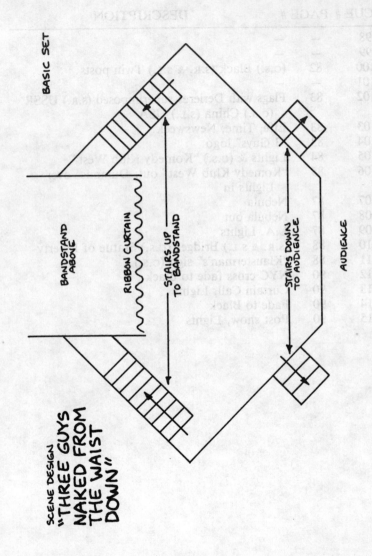

SCENE DESIGN
"THREE GUYS NAKED FROM THE WAIST DOWN"

BASIC SET

AUDIENCE

BANDSTAND ABOVE

RIBBON CURTAIN

STAIRS UP TO BANDSTAND

STAIRS DOWN TO AUDIENCE

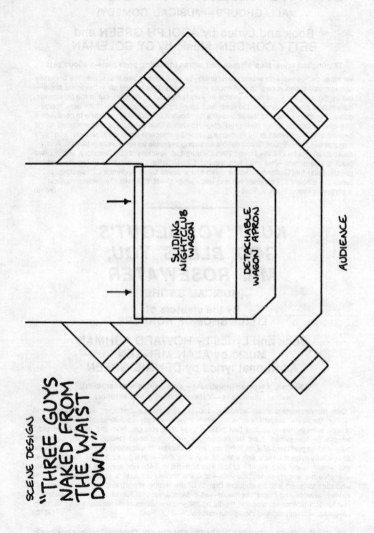

ON THE TWENTIETH CENTURY

(ALL GROUPS—MUSICAL COMEDY)

Book and Lyrics by ADOLPH GREEN and BETTY COMDEN, Music by CY COLEMAN

17 principal roles, plus singers and extras (doubling possible)—Various sets

Whether performed with elaborate scenery, or on a simple skeletal scale, this brilliantly comic musical can appeal to audiences everywhere. This is truly an extravagant show—but its extravagance lies not in its scenery and physical production, but in the boisterous, tumultuous energy—and in the lush and sprightly energetic surge of its very melodic score. The story concerns the efforts of a flamboyant theatrical impressario to persuade a film star to appear in his next production, to outwit rival producers and creditors, to rid himself of religious nut Letitia Primrose (played by Imogene Coca on Broadway) and Lily's film star boyfriend Bruce Granit (who's as strong in profile as he is weak in brains). And, he must do all this before the famed 20th Century Ltd. reaches NYC! The story, and it's two leading characters—the mad impressario Oscar Jaffe and the love of his life and his greatest star Lily Garland—can be loved and enjoyed by all audiences. "Spectacular . . . funny . . . elegant . . . civilized wit and wild humor."—N.Y. Times. "A perfect musical . . . a gorgeous show! "—N.Y. Post. (#819)

KURT VONNEGUT'S GOD BLESS YOU, MR. ROSEWATER

(MUSICAL SATIRE)

By the creators of LITTLE SHOP OF HORRORS

Book and Lyrics by HOWARD ASHMAN
Music by ALAN MENKEN
Additional lyrics by DENNIS GREEN

10 men, 4 women (principals—also double smaller roles), extras, musicians—Various interiors and exteriors

"One of Vonnegut's most affecting and likeable novels becomes an affecting and likable theatrical experience, with more inventiveness, cockeyed characters, high-muzzle-velocity dialogue and just plain energy that you get from the majority of playwrights."—Newsweek. Eliot Rosewater's a well-intentioned idealist and philanthropic nut—and as president of a multi-million family foundation dispenses money to arcane and artsy-crafty projects. He's also a World War II veteran with a guilt complex, haunted by all this wealth—and also slightly crazy. His outlandish behavior enrages his senator dad, alienates his society-conscious wife—and the money attracts a young, shyster lawyer who tries to divert it to an obscure branch of the family. It portrays Vonnegut's vision of money, avarice and human behavior—as it aims a satrical fusillade at plastic America, fast foods, trademarks, slogans, media blitzes and the follies of materialism. "A charming, delightful, unexpected and thoughtful musical."—N.Y. Post. (#630)

Other Publications for Your Interest

PUMP BOYS AND DINETTES
(ALL GROUPS—MUSICAL)

By JOHN FOLEY, MARK HARDWICK,
DEBRA MONK, CASS MORGAN,
JOHN SCHIMMEL and JIM WANN

4 men, 2 women—Composite interior

This delightful little show went from Off Off Broadway to Off Broadway to Broadway, where it had a long run. This is an evening of country/western songs performed by the actors—on guitars, piano, bass and, yes, kitchen utensils. There are the four Pump Boys: L.M. on the Piano (singing such delights as "The Night Dolly Parton Was Almost Mine"), Jim on rhythm guitar (the spokesman of the Pump Boys), Jackson on lead guitar (whose rocker about Mona, a check-out girl at Woolworth's, stops the show) and Eddie, who plays bass. The Dinettes are Prudie and Rhetta Cupp, who run the Double Cupp Diner across from the Pump Boys' gas station. "Totally delightful . . . the easiest, chummiest, happiest show in town."—Newsweek. "Totally terrific."—N.Y. Post. "It tickles the funny bone and makes everybody feel, just for the evening, like a good ole boy or a good ole girl."—Time. "It doesn't merely celebrate the value of friendship and life's simple pleasures, it embodies them."—N.Y. Times.   (#18135)

GOLD DUST
(ALL GROUPS—MUSICAL)

Book by JON JORY
Music and Lyrics by JIM WANN

5 men, 3 women, 3 piece combo—Interior

Set in a saloon in a western mining camp in the 1850's, *Gold Dust* is a *very* loose musical adaptation of Molière's *The Miser*. The story concerns a prospector named Jebediah Harp who has hit it rich and hoards his gold. Perfect for high schools, colleges and community theatres, this is another hit from Louisville's famed Actors Theater. The music and lyrics are by the very talented Jim Wann, whose other works include *Pump Boys and Dinettes*, *Diamond Studs* and *Hot Grog*. "It's spunky and raucous, clangorous and tuneful. It overflows with a theatrical zest that is pretty much irresistible."—Louisville Courier Journal. ". . . the small musical that budget-minded theatres across the land have been praying for."—Louisville Times. "Best of all is Wann's music, a mixture of jazz, blues, rock, folk and country-western styles."—Variety.   (#9134)

Other Publications for Your Interest

A ... MY NAME IS ALICE
(LITTLE THEATRE—REVUE)
Conceived by JOAN MICKLIN SILVER
and JULIANNE BOYD

5 women—Bare stage with set pieces

This terrific new show definitely rates an "A"—in fact, an "A-*plus*"! Originally produced by the Women's Project at the American Place Theatre in New York City, "Alice" settled down for a long run at the Village Gate, off Broadway. When you hear the songs, and read the sketches, you'll know why. The music runs the gamut from blues to torch to rock to wistful easy listening. There are hilarious songs, such as "Honeypot" (about a Black blues singer who can only sing about sex euphemistically) and heartbreakingly beautiful numbers such as "I Sure Like the Boys". A ... *My Name is Alice* is a feminist revue in the best sense. It could charm even the most die-hard male chauvinist. "Delightful . . . the music and lyrics are so sophisticated that they can carry the weight of one-act plays".—NY Times. "Bright, party-time, pick-me-up stuff . . . Bouncy music, witty patter, and a bundle of laughs".—NY Post.   (#3647)

I'M GETTING MY ACT TOGETHER AND TAKING IT ON THE ROAD
(ALL GROUPS—MUSICAL)
Book and Lyrics by GRETCHEN CRYER
Music by NANCY FORD

6 men, 4 women—Bare stage

This new musical by the authors of *The Last Sweet Days of Isaac* was a hit at Joseph Papp's Public Theatre and transferred to the Circle-in-the-Square theatre in New York for a successful off-Broadway run. It is about a 40-year-old song writer who wants to make a come-back. The central conflict is between the song writer and her manager. She wants to include feminist material in her act—he wants her to go back to the syrupy-sweet, non-controversial formula which was once successful. "Clearly the most imaginative and melodic score heard in New York all season."—Soho Weekly News. "Brash, funny, very agreeable in its brash and funny way, and moreover, it touches a special emotional chord for our times."—N.Y. Post.   (#11025)